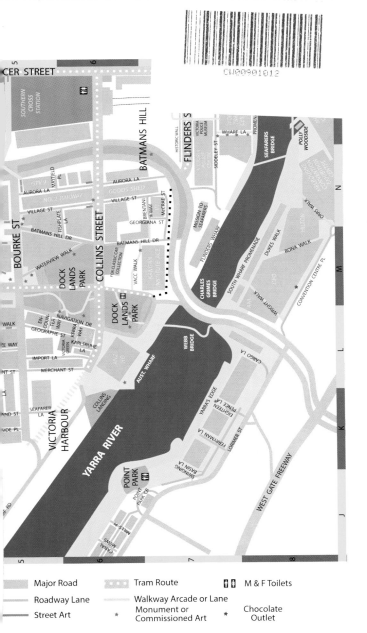

CER STREET

SOUTHERN CROSS STATION

BATMANS HILL

FLINDERS S

HISTORIC WALL

VICTORIA POLICE MUSEUM

WHARF LA

PROMEN

SEAFARERS BRIDGE

POLLY WOODSIDE

MAYFIELD PL

CITY RD

AURORA LA

NO.2 RAILWAY

GOODS SHED

AURORA LA

VILLAGE ST

VILLAGE ST

FISHPLATE LA

BATMANS HILL DR

COLLINS STREET

BOURKE ST

SIDDELEY ST

BRENTANI WAY

McCRAE ST

MISSION TO SEAFARERS

WHARF LA

GEORGIANA ST

WATERVIEW WALK

BATMANS HILL DR

FLINDERS WHARF

DOCK LANDS PARK

FORCLASSIC CAR COLLECTION

VACC WALK

KEREN INSTITUTE PL

CHARLES GRIMES BRIDGE

SOUTH WHARF PROMENADE

DUKES WALK

RONA WALK

WILTON

OHIO WALK

WALK

EZE WAY

EN COUN TER WAY

NAVIGATION DR

GEOGRAPHE ST

KERRA LA

KARLSRUHE LA

DOCK LANDS PARK

WEBB BRIDGE

CARGO LA

WRIGHT WALK

CONVENTION CENTRE PL

NT ST

AND ST

IMPORT LA

MERCHANT ST

AUST WHARF

VICTORIA HARBOUR

SEAFARER LA

SIDE PL

COLLINS LANDING

YARRA'S EDGE

EIGHTEEN FENCE LA

FERRMANN LA

LORIMER ST

CARGO LA

YARRA RIVER

RK RD

POINT PARK

POINT PARK DR

SWINNING BASIN LA

WEST GATE FREEWAY

CANAL MEWS

MILLS PL

	Major Road		Tram Route	🚹 🚻	M & F Toilets
	Roadway Lane		Walkway Arcade or Lane		
	Street Art	✷	Monument or Commissioned Art	✷	Chocolate Outlet

MAPS

Laneways

— of —

Melbourne

2nd Edition

*There are many secret and hidden delights
waiting to be discovered
in Melbourne's laneways.*

M

MELBOURNE BOOKS

Introduction

*M*elbourne's unique arcades and laneways are a mecca for people who love to explore, socialise, shop and eat. Fashionable boutiques, coffee and cake shops, tearooms, bars, restaurants and alfresco dining enhance a warm street ambience enjoyed by many.

Walking along the main streets of Melbourne, you will bypass the lanes and hidden treasures of the city.

Surveyor Robert Hoddle (1794–1881) designed the street grid (Hoddle's Grid) of Melbourne's Central Business District in 1837. The wide streets allowed bullock carts to ride through Melbourne's centre. Laneways permeated the city blocks to be used for workshops, deliveries, factories, rubbish disposal, public urinals and brothels, and were often associated with vice and crime.

The stories are fascinating, and many buildings, warehouses and cobbled bluestone streets can still be visited.

Today the arcades and laneways, alleys and small streets of Melbourne remain wonderful places of excitement and discovery.

Laneways of Melbourne presents vibrant street art, fascinating history, secret locations, popular restaurants, chocolate and cake shops, cafés, clubs and much more.

Centre Place

ACDC Lane

The lane is named after the legendary Australian rock band AC/DC. It runs south of Flinders Lane, between Russell and Exhibition streets (G5).

Street art is present in the lane.

The Cherry Bar

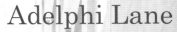

Adelphi Lane

While this unnamed lane may not look special, it is a good example of the hidden secrets that can be discovered in Melbourne's laneways.

It is located between Swanston and Russell streets, south of Flinders Lane (F5).

The nearby Anna Schwartz Gallery showcases contemporary art.

Image courtesy of Mon Bijou

The breathtaking Mon Bijou penthouse function space has panoramic views of Melbourne's skyline.

Adelphi Hotel   art@Adelphi   Ezard at Adelphi   Mon Bijou

Albert Coates Lane

The lane is part of the Queen Victoria Melbourne (QV) complex. It is located between Swanston and Russell streets, and Lonsdale and Little Lonsdale streets (F2).

Sir Albert Coates OBE, in the 1920s, was a surgeon at the Royal Melbourne Hospital. He served in Gallipoli in 1915, and during World War II in Singapore and Java, where he was captured. He treated those in need on the Burma–Thailand railway.

Romano's Coffee

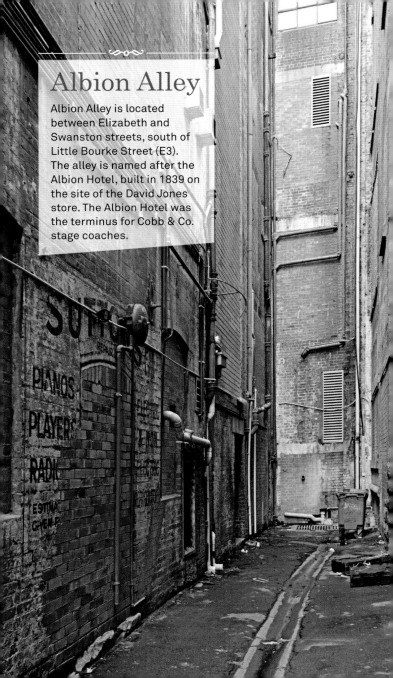

Albion Alley

Albion Alley is located between Elizabeth and Swanston streets, south of Little Bourke Street (E3). The alley is named after the Albion Hotel, built in 1839 on the site of the David Jones store. The Albion Hotel was the terminus for Cobb & Co. stage coaches.

Alfred Place

Alfred Place is located between Russell and Exhibition streets, connecting Collins Street to Little Collins Street (G4). During the 1860s, doctors, dentists, boarding houses and a school for ladies occupied the lane. Alfred Place was possibly named after Prince Alfred, then Duke of Edinburgh, who visited Australia in 1867.

Sir Stamford Raffles was the British visionary who founded Singapore in 1819.

Comme was built in 1885 as The German Club and was a preferred lecture venue of eminent botanist Baron von Mueller.

Comme   Harry's Bar & Restaurant

Massoni Wine Bar   Stamford Plaza Melbourne Hotel

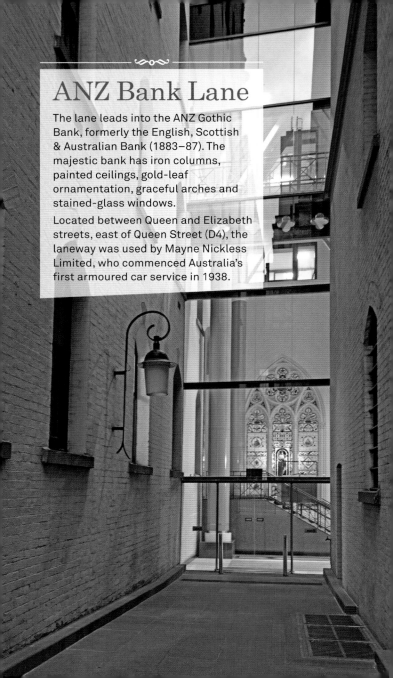

ANZ Bank Lane

The lane leads into the ANZ Gothic Bank, formerly the English, Scottish & Australian Bank (1883–87). The majestic bank has iron columns, painted ceilings, gold-leaf ornamentation, graceful arches and stained-glass windows.

Located between Queen and Elizabeth streets, east of Queen Street (D4), the laneway was used by Mayne Nickless Limited, who commenced Australia's first armoured car service in 1938.

Aquarium Drive

Aquarium Drive is located between William and King streets, south of Flinders Street (B6). The drive separates Melbourne Aquarium, one of Australia's premier tourist attractions, from Enterprize Park, which features a 20-metre flagpole with the City of Melbourne flag, the 'Scar Project' (various scarred trees), a ship's propeller and access to Enterprize Wharf.

Also situated here is the Flinders Street Viaduct (1891).

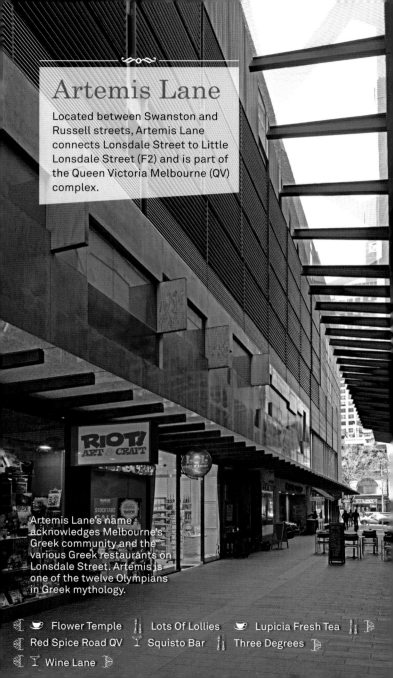

Artemis Lane

Located between Swanston and Russell streets, Artemis Lane connects Lonsdale Street to Little Lonsdale Street (F2) and is part of the Queen Victoria Melbourne (QV) complex.

Artemis Lane's name acknowledges Melbourne's Greek community and the various Greek restaurants on Lonsdale Street. Artemis is one of the twelve Olympians in Greek mythology.

Flower Temple   Lots Of Lollies   Lupicia Fresh Tea

Red Spice Road QV   Squisto Bar   Three Degrees

Wine Lane

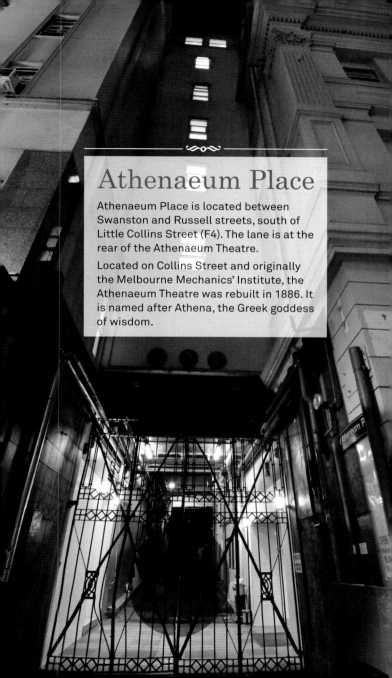

Athenaeum Place

Athenaeum Place is located between Swanston and Russell streets, south of Little Collins Street (F4). The lane is at the rear of the Athenaeum Theatre.

Located on Collins Street and originally the Melbourne Mechanics' Institute, the Athenaeum Theatre was rebuilt in 1886. It is named after Athena, the Greek goddess of wisdom.

Austral Lane

Austral Lane is located between William and Queen streets, south of Little Collins Street (C4). It is possibly named after the Bank of Australasia or the Australian Club, both of which are nearby.

Aki Sushi

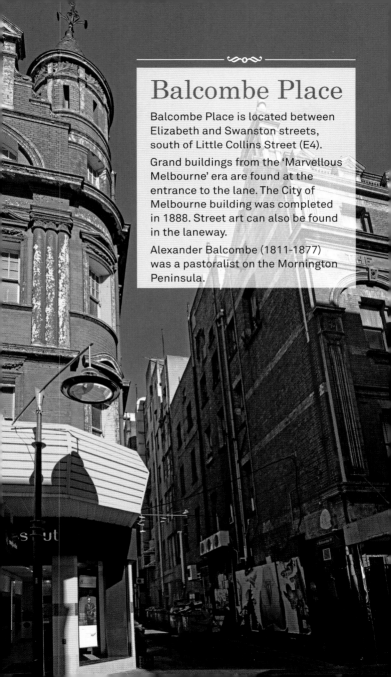

Balcombe Place

Balcombe Place is located between Elizabeth and Swanston streets, south of Little Collins Street (E4).

Grand buildings from the 'Marvellous Melbourne' era are found at the entrance to the lane. The City of Melbourne building was completed in 1888. Street art can also be found in the laneway.

Alexander Balcombe (1811-1877) was a pastoralist on the Mornington Peninsula.

Banana Alley

Banana Alley is located on the north bank of the Yarra River, west of Flinders Street Station (C6).

The Banana Alley vaults were built in 1891 and stored produce before transportation to markets. Bananas stored in the vaults gave the alley its name.

T-Roy Browns Café

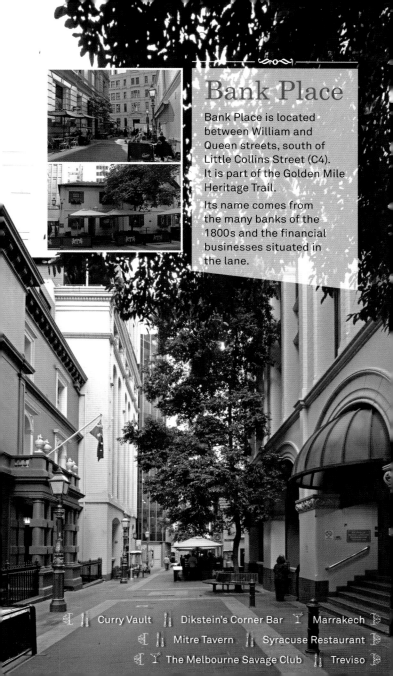

Bank Place

Bank Place is located between William and Queen streets, south of Little Collins Street (C4). It is part of the Golden Mile Heritage Trail.

Its name comes from the many banks of the 1800s and the financial businesses situated in the lane.

Curry Vault   Dikstein's Corner Bar   Marrakech

Mitre Tavern   Syracuse Restaurant

The Melbourne Savage Club   Treviso

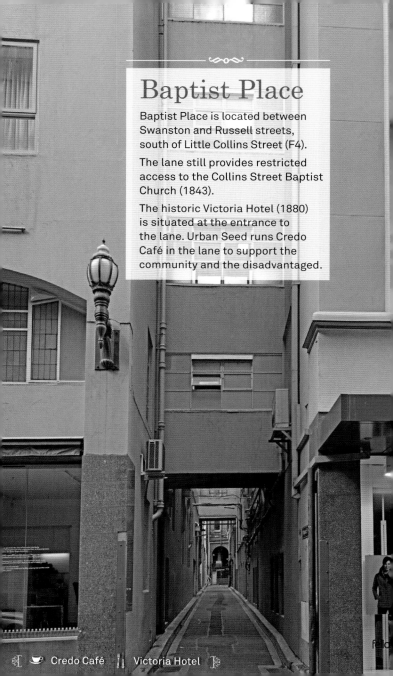

Baptist Place

Baptist Place is located between Swanston and Russell streets, south of Little Collins Street (F4).

The lane still provides restricted access to the Collins Street Baptist Church (1843).

The historic Victoria Hotel (1880) is situated at the entrance to the lane. Urban Seed runs Credo Café in the lane to support the community and the disadvantaged.

Credo Café   Victoria Hotel

Barry Lane

Barry Lane is located between William and Queen streets, joining Little Bourke Street to Lonsdale Street (C3).

The lane was previously called Tankards Place after John Tankard, who ran the Temperance Hotel, a grand place to socialise without the 'evils of alcohol'. Its current namesake, Sir Redmond Barry (1813-1880), was a judge at the nearby Supreme Court.

Wunderkammer (scientific curiosities, artefacts & ephemera) is found at the entrance to the lane.

Mr Burger

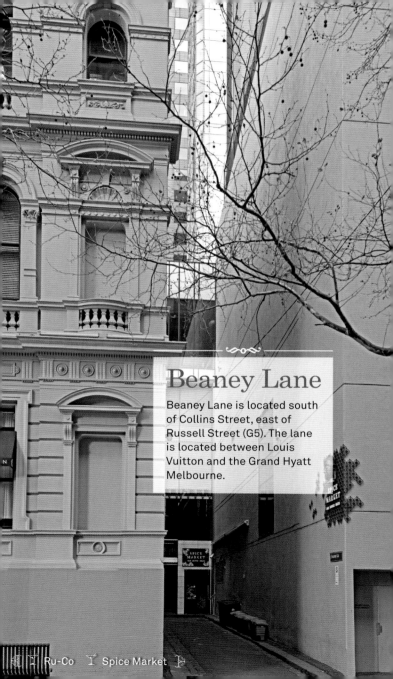

Beaney Lane

Beaney Lane is located south of Collins Street, east of Russell Street (G5). The lane is located between Louis Vuitton and the Grand Hyatt Melbourne.

Ru-Co   Spice Market

Bell Place

Located between Russell and Exhibition streets, Bell Place leads north from La Trobe Street (G1).

The bluestone lane and building hint at the old age of the area. In 1905, the lane was associated with a blacksmith's shop and coach building works.

Bennetts Lane

Bennetts Lane is located between Russell and Exhibition streets, north of Little Lonsdale Street (G2).

The lane is named after Robert Bennett MLA (1822-1891), mayor of Melbourne from 1861 to 1862. Bennetts Lane Jazz Club and Ruby's Music Room can be found here.

Bennetts Lane Jazz Club hosts international artists including Herbie Hancock and Prince, as well as the best local jazz artists like Paul Grabowski, Allan Browne and Aaron Choulai.

Benson Lane

Benson Lane leads west off Exhibition Street, north of Collins Street (G4).

Tattersalls Horse Bazaar, owned by John Black, was situated here during the late 1800s. Today, the popular lane is lined with trees and a mix of old and new architecture.

The lane continues to Collins Street, past the mural *Melbourne: Two Worlds* by the Wurundjeri community artists Judy Nicholson, James MacFayden, Ashley Firebrace-Kerr and Derek Smith.

Collins Quarter is situated at the end of the lane, which has walkways around the 80 Collins Street building.

The former townhouse and surgery (1867) adjacent to the lane are examples of the townhouses that existed in this area in the 1800s.

Collins Quarter

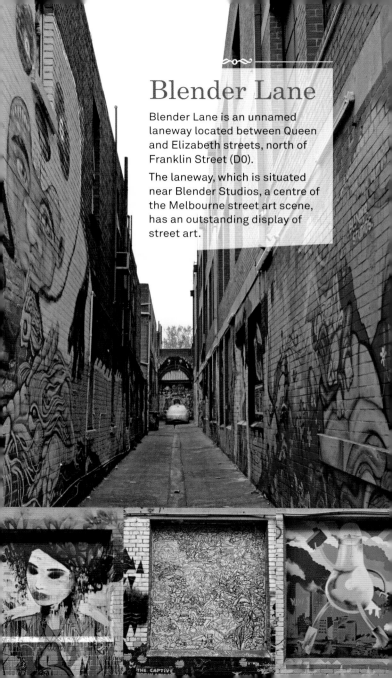

Blender Lane

Blender Lane is an unnamed laneway located between Queen and Elizabeth streets, north of Franklin Street (D0).

The laneway, which is situated near Blender Studios, a centre of the Melbourne street art scene, has an outstanding display of street art.

Bligh Place

Bligh Place is located between Queen and Elizabeth streets, opposite Victoria University, north of Flinders Lane (D5).

Merchants Bligh & Harbottle operated a warehouse in Flinders Lane, from the 1860s.

Bistro du Monde   Café Frais   Hako Japanese Restaurant

Leicester House   Milé Café Bar   Robot Sushi & Bar

The Deanery

Block Arcade

This historic arcade is one of Melbourne's icons and is located on the corner of Collins and Elizabeth streets (E4). Completed in 1892, it was modelled after the style of the Galleria Vittorio Emmanuele in Milan, Italy.

Its name comes from the 1870s tradition of 'Doing the Block', whereby crowds visited the prestigious shops in the vicinity.

☕ Caffé Duomo   ☕ Haigh's Chocolates   ☕ Hopetoun Tea Rooms

Briscoes Bulk Grain Store occupied the site from 1856 to 1883, followed by the Georges and Georges Federation Emporium until a spectacular fire in 1889. The bluestone footings for the current building came from the Briscoes store. The Block Arcade was developed by financier Benjamin Fink and the City Property & Co. Pty Ltd at a cost of £46,233.

The Singer Sewing Machine Company set up their prestigious store in the Block Arcade in 1902. In 1907, artist Phillip Goatcher (1852–1931) painted a mural showing the scientific advances of Astronomy, Chemistry, Electricity and Mathematics, as well as a lady holding the Singer Sewing Machine logo. The Crabtree & Evelyn shop displays the mural.

Wittner's Shoes displays a pressed metal ceiling, installed by the first Kodak shop in Melbourne over 100 years ago.

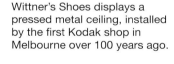

The arcade has a glass roof with a glass dome at its corner. Skylights and stained-glass windows are used throughout the building.

The beautiful mosaic tile floor was Australia's largest area of mosaics at the time of its construction. The classic Victorian design is made from Italian tiles.

At the Elizabeth Street entrance, the 1927 staircase leads to what was first tenanted as the Winter Garden Tea Rooms, now the auction rooms of Downies Coins & Collectables.

The basement, dating to 1856 from Briscoes Bulk Grain Store, has been utilised as part of the arcade.

Haigh's Chocolates displays The Tapping Man, a German-made mechanical doll. The doll was displayed in L. P. Alexander's tailoring store at 214 Swanston Street from the 1930s to the 1970s. Now restored, The Tapping Man continues to delight Melbourne shoppers.

The Hopetoun Tea Rooms were opened in 1892 by the Victorian Ladies' Work Association. They were named after the association's founder, Lady Hopetoun, the wife of Lord Hopetoun, Victoria's first Governor. The tearooms contain a magnificent mirror with the year 1891 etched at the top.

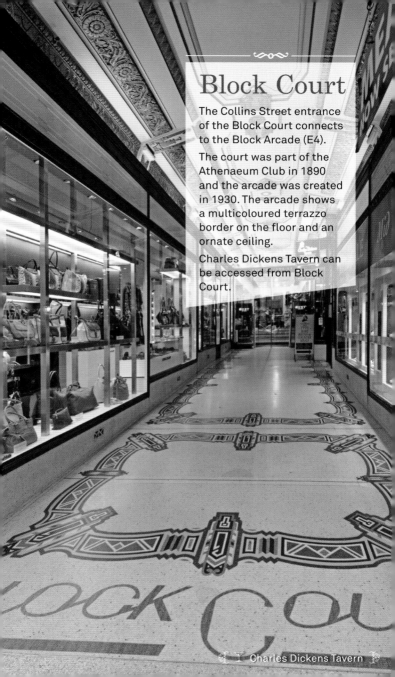

Block Court

The Collins Street entrance of the Block Court connects to the Block Arcade (E4).

The court was part of the Athenaeum Club in 1890 and the arcade was created in 1930. The arcade shows a multicoloured terrazzo border on the floor and an ornate ceiling.

Charles Dickens Tavern can be accessed from Block Court.

Charles Dickens Tavern

Block Place

The lane is joined to the Block Arcade and connects to Bourke Street (E4).

This popular pedestrian laneway contains intimate cafés and shops.

Brown Sugar Café · Café Segovia · C&B Café e Biscotti

Dinkum Pies · Haigh's Chocolates · Olio Cucina

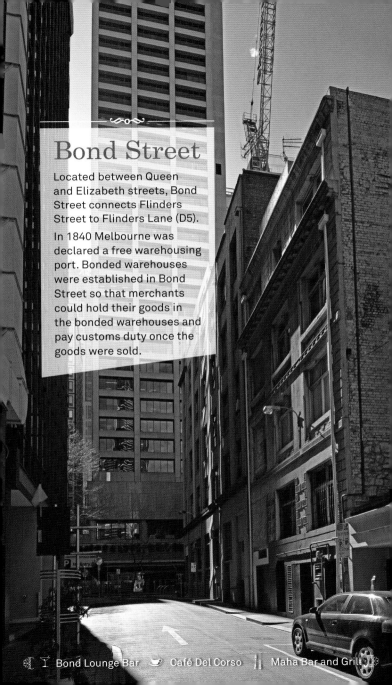

Bond Street

Located between Queen and Elizabeth streets, Bond Street connects Flinders Street to Flinders Lane (D5).

In 1840 Melbourne was declared a free warehousing port. Bonded warehouses were established in Bond Street so that merchants could hold their goods in the bonded warehouses and pay customs duty once the goods were sold.

Bond Lounge Bar   Café Del Corso   Maha Bar and Grill

Bourke Place

Bourke Place leads east from King Street into the Bourke Place Office Tower on the corner of Bourke and King streets (B3). Nando's, Vivace and the Bourke Place arcade can be accessed via the lane.

Blufish   Burger Edge   Kedai Satay   la di da

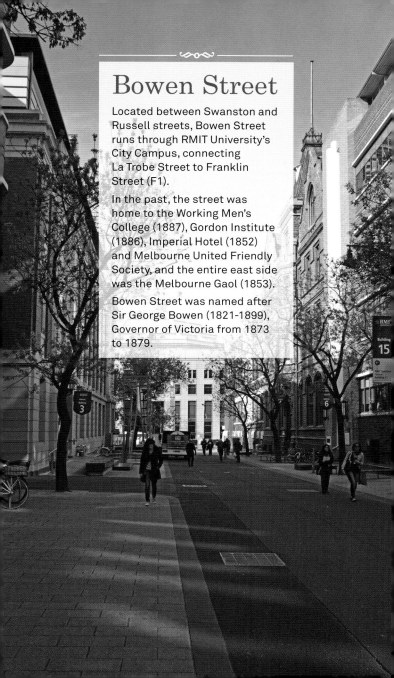

Bowen Street

Located between Swanston and Russell streets, Bowen Street runs through RMIT University's City Campus, connecting La Trobe Street to Franklin Street (F1).

In the past, the street was home to the Working Men's College (1887), Gordon Institute (1886), Imperial Hotel (1852) and Melbourne United Friendly Society, and the entire east side was the Melbourne Gaol (1853).

Bowen Street was named after Sir George Bowen (1821-1899), Governor of Victoria from 1873 to 1879.

Brien Lane

This narrow lane is located between Russell and Exhibition streets, north of Bourke Street towards Little Bourke Street (G3). It was named in 1872 after Joseph Brien, a butcher who lived in the area in 1848.

The coloured pavement areas are the remains of Louisa Bufardeci's 2001 artwork *There are a few facts I think you ought to know.*

F.M Karaoke & Bar   Ginza Tepanyaki   Shark Fin House

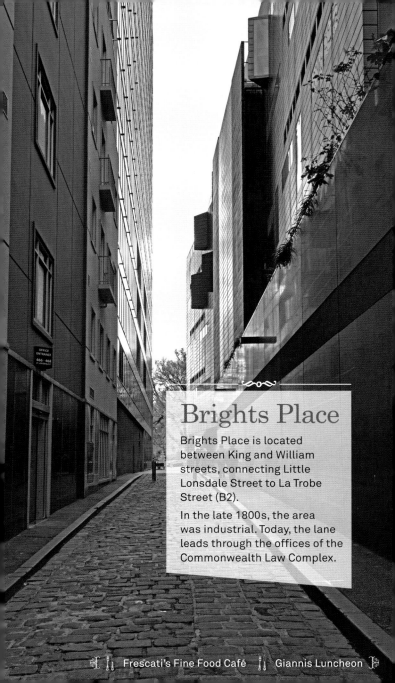

Brights Place

Brights Place is located between King and William streets, connecting Little Lonsdale Street to La Trobe Street (B2).

In the late 1800s, the area was industrial. Today, the lane leads through the offices of the Commonwealth Law Complex.

Frescati's Fine Food Café | Giannis Luncheon

Brown Alley

Brown Alley is located between King and William streets, north of Little Bourke Street (B3). Brown Boy Inn operated here in 1860 and likely gave the alley its name. The Lonsdale Street end of the alley is bordered by the elegant 1858 bluestone Cleve Brothers warehouse (Seabrook House) and the Colonial Hotel.

Brown Alley

Colonial Hotel   Great Western Hotel

Bullens Lane

Bullens Lane is located between Swanston and Russell streets, connecting Russell and Little Bourke streets (F3).

The lane is named after Frederick Bullen & Son, who operated a clothing store in Little Bourke Street in the 1880s.

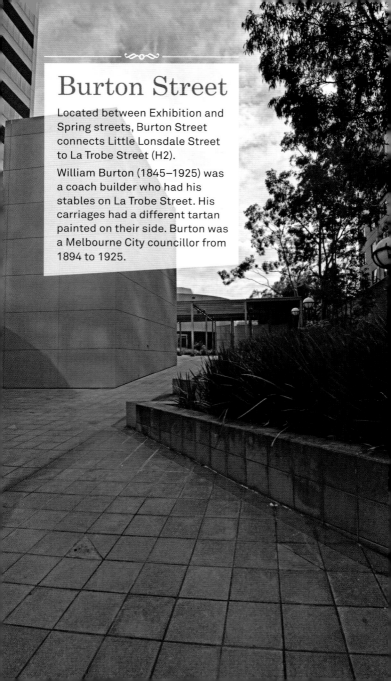

Burton Street

Located between Exhibition and Spring streets, Burton Street connects Little Lonsdale Street to La Trobe Street (H2).

William Burton (1845–1925) was a coach builder who had his stables on La Trobe Street. His carriages had a different tartan painted on their side. Burton was a Melbourne City councillor from 1894 to 1925.

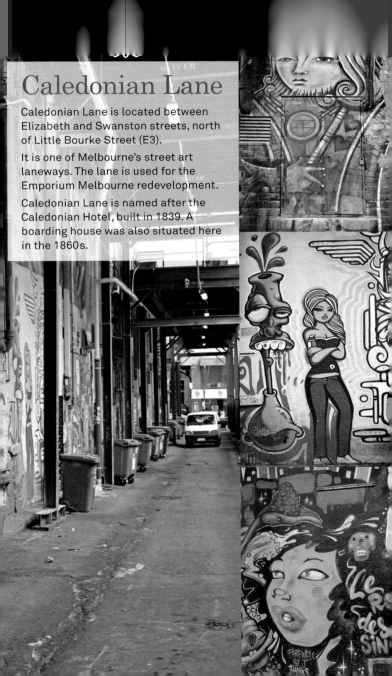

Caledonian Lane

Caledonian Lane is located between Elizabeth and Swanston streets, north of Little Bourke Street (E3).

It is one of Melbourne's street art laneways. The lane is used for the Emporium Melbourne redevelopment.

Caledonian Lane is named after the Caledonian Hotel, built in 1839. A boarding house was also situated here in the 1860s.

Campbell Arcade

Also known as the Degraves Street Subway, the arcade links Degraves Street to Flinders Street Station (E6). The arcade was opened in 1955 for the 1956 Melbourne Summer Olympics.

Shops in the arcade include Corky Saint Clair, Cup of Truth, Some Like It Hot Consignment, PC Repair & Internet Access, Sticky Institute, Subject to Change, Subway Newsagency, The Cats Meow, Touch of Paris Hair and Wax Museum Records.

The arcade shows what Melbourne looked like in the 1950s. A passage in the arcade, which once led into the Mutual Store, is now closed, as is the alcove of telephone boxes.

The Art Deco arcade with black marble columns and pink-tiled walls has 13 exhibition display cases, which showcase the work of artists. This is run by Platform Artists Group Inc. and commenced in 1990.

Cup of Truth

Capitol Arcade

The arcade is located between Collins and Little Collins streets and leads west from Swanston Street (E4). It is named after the Capitol Theatre, which opened in 1924.

The Capitol Theatre was designed by Walter Burley Griffin and his wife, Marion Mahony, and opened in 1924.

The theatre is considered an architectural masterpiece.

Delicious Delights Phillippa's Thai Viet Bibigo

Carson Place

This modest-looking lane is located between Elizabeth and Swanston streets, south of Little Collins Street (E4). The lane is likely named after Carsons Quality Footwear, whose elaborate façade was a feature of the lane. John Carson, in the 1840s, imported boots and shoes.

Casselden Place

Casselden Place is located between Exhibition and Spring streets, south of Little Lonsdale Street (H2). The lane connects to Madame Brussells Lane.

In the 1850s, the 'Little Lon' district was a working-class area with simple houses, small businesses and later a few factories.

Commonwealth Offices are now situated at Casselden Place.

This house is the last of six two-room brick cottages built in 1877 by John Casselden, who was a shoemaker and developer.

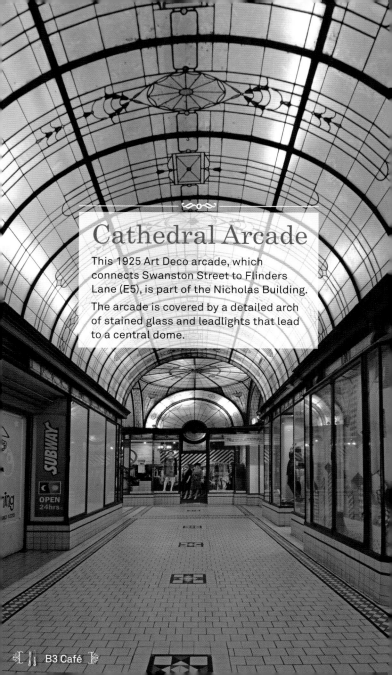

Cathedral Arcade

This 1925 Art Deco arcade, which connects Swanston Street to Flinders Lane (E5), is part of the Nicholas Building.

The arcade is covered by a detailed arch of stained glass and leadlights that lead to a central dome.

B3 Café

Celestial Avenue

This avenue runs north of Little Bourke Street in Chinatown (F3). By 1860, it was the site of many Chinese boarding houses.

Many settlers came from the See Yap (Four Districts) area of Guangdong province, China. 'Celestial' was a term used to refer to Chinese immigrants, as the sons of China's 'Celestial Empire'.

Heyday Hong Kong Café   Supper Inn   The Crane Restaurant

Yang Guang Café

Centre Place

Centre Place is located between Elizabeth and Swanston streets, north of Flinders Lane (E5).

This busy lane is lined with boutiques, cafés and restaurants. It branches to the west, where street art is prolific.

Aix Café Creperie Salon   B3 Café et Patisserie

Blufish   Café No. 5   Centro Espresso Caffe

Grind in the City   Hell's Kitchen   In A Rush   Issus

Jungle Juice Bar   Lorca   Lustre Bar

The Soup Place   Vicolino   Yen Sushi & Noodles   Yen Bar

Melbourne's street art is world-renowned and a unique city attraction.

Pictured is some of the street art at Centre Place.

Centreway Arcade

The arcade is located between Elizabeth and Swanston streets, north of Flinders Lane, past Centre Place (E5).

The building and arcade were built in 1912. At the southern end of the arcade, a wall of letters displays a seldom-read message:

We live in a society that sets an inordinate value on consumer goods and services.

Delight Sandwich Bar | Health Cosmos | Matsuki

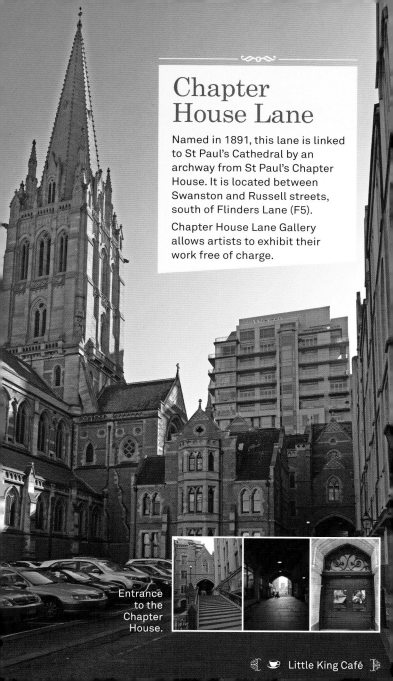

Chapter House Lane

Named in 1891, this lane is linked to St Paul's Cathedral by an archway from St Paul's Chapter House. It is located between Swanston and Russell streets, south of Flinders Lane (F5).

Chapter House Lane Gallery allows artists to exhibit their work free of charge.

Entrance to the Chapter House.

Little King Café

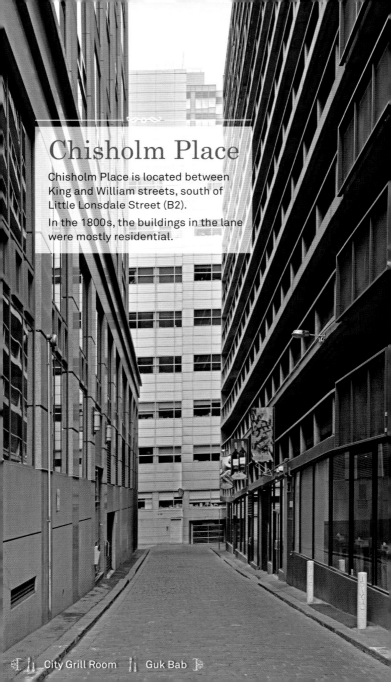

Chisholm Place

Chisholm Place is located between King and William streets, south of Little Lonsdale Street (B2).

In the 1800s, the buildings in the lane were mostly residential.

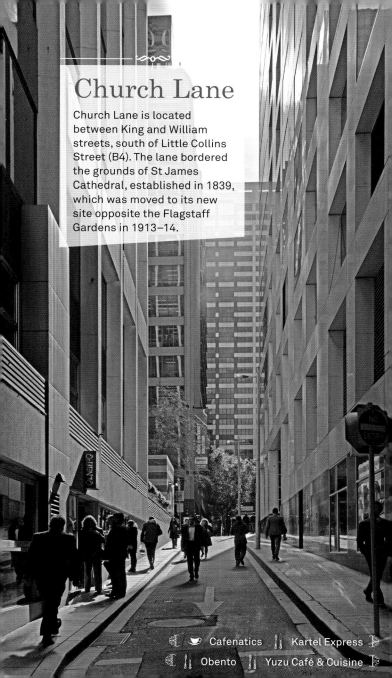

Church Lane

Church Lane is located between King and William streets, south of Little Collins Street (B4). The lane bordered the grounds of St James Cathedral, established in 1839, which was moved to its new site opposite the Flagstaff Gardens in 1913–14.

Cafenatics   Kartel Express

Obento   Yuzu Café & Cuisine

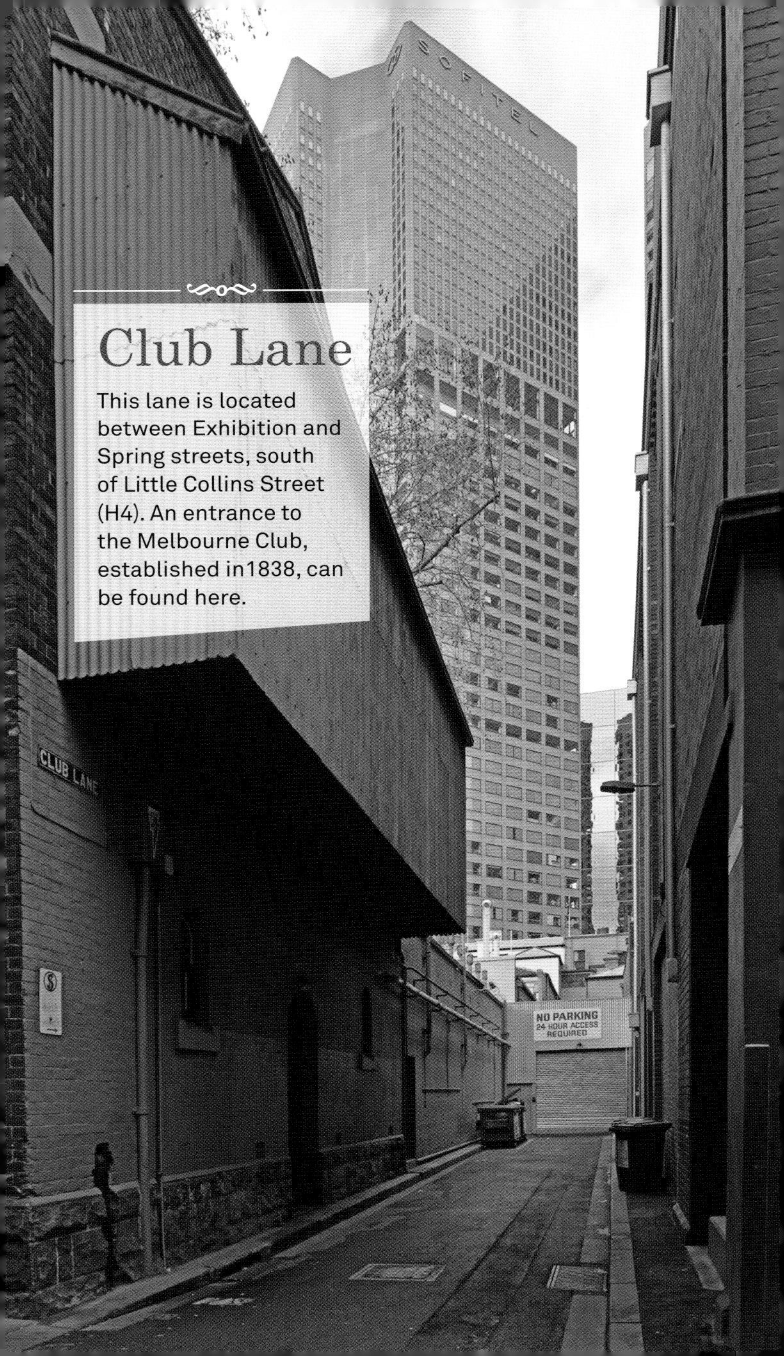
SOFITEL
CLUB LANE
NO PARKING
24 HOUR ACCESS
REQUIRED

Club Lane

This lane is located between Exhibition and Spring streets, south of Little Collins Street (H4). An entrance to the Melbourne Club, established in1838, can be found here.

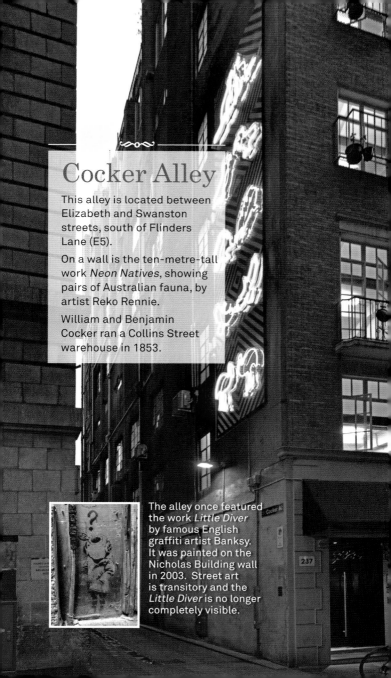

Cocker Alley

This alley is located between Elizabeth and Swanston streets, south of Flinders Lane (E5).

On a wall is the ten-metre-tall work *Neon Natives*, showing pairs of Australian fauna, by artist Reko Rennie.

William and Benjamin Cocker ran a Collins Street warehouse in 1853.

The alley once featured the work *Little Diver* by famous English graffiti artist Banksy. It was painted on the Nicholas Building wall in 2003. Street art is transitory and the *Little Diver* is no longer completely visible.

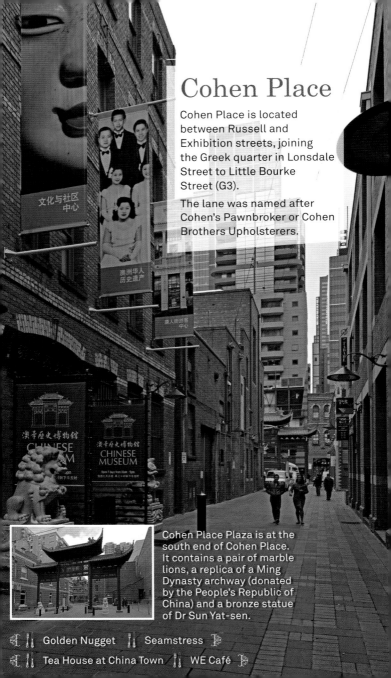

Cohen Place

Cohen Place is located between Russell and Exhibition streets, joining the Greek quarter in Lonsdale Street to Little Bourke Street (G3).

The lane was named after Cohen's Pawnbroker or Cohen Brothers Upholsterers.

Cohen Place Plaza is at the south end of Cohen Place. It contains a pair of marble lions, a replica of a Ming Dynasty archway (donated by the People's Republic of China) and a bronze statue of Dr Sun Yat-sen.

Golden Nugget · Seamstress
Tea House at China Town · WE Café

Collins Way

Collins Way is located between Queen and Elizabeth streets, south of Little Collins Street (D4).

The historic Collins Gate is an apartment building.

COLLINS GATE

Nori Nori

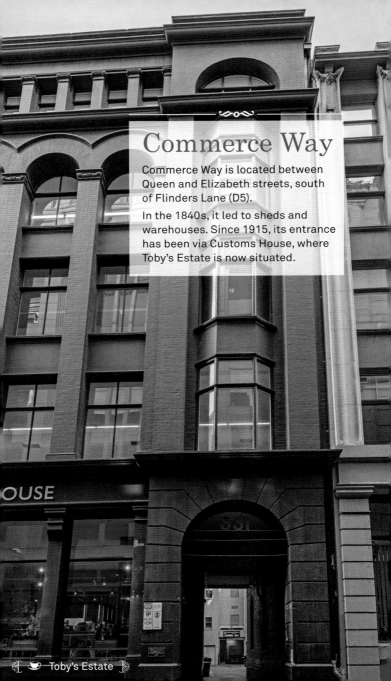

Commerce Way

Commerce Way is located between Queen and Elizabeth streets, south of Flinders Lane (D5).

In the 1840s, it led to sheds and warehouses. Since 1915, its entrance has been via Customs House, where Toby's Estate is now situated.

Toby's Estate

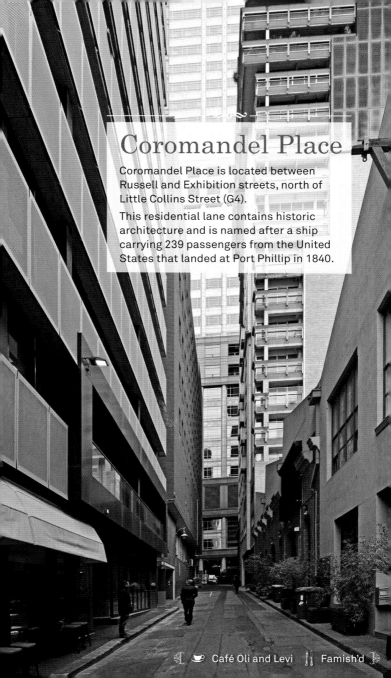

Coromandel Place

Coromandel Place is located between Russell and Exhibition streets, north of Little Collins Street (G4).

This residential lane contains historic architecture and is named after a ship carrying 239 passengers from the United States that landed at Port Phillip in 1840.

Café Oli and Levi | Famish'd

Corrs Lane

A lane in Chinatown, Corrs Lane is located between Russell and Exhibition streets, north of Little Bourke Street (G3).

In the 1890s, Alcocks manufactured billiard tables here.

Street art

Ants Bistro   Berlin Bar   Brutale   Dhaka Restaurant

Dragon Boat Palace   Fad Gallery   House of Maximon

Sichuan House   Yamato

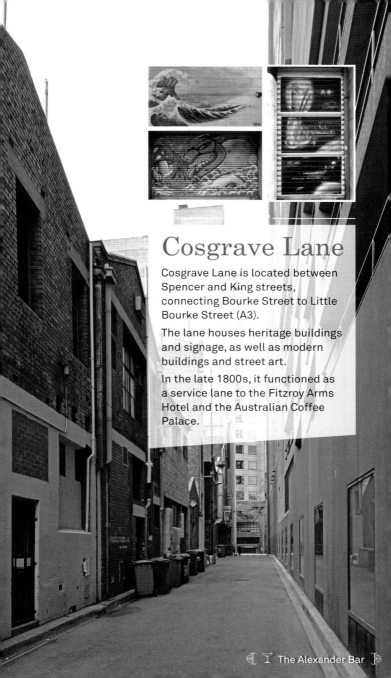

Cosgrave Lane

Cosgrave Lane is located between Spencer and King streets, connecting Bourke Street to Little Bourke Street (A3).

The lane houses heritage buildings and signage, as well as modern buildings and street art.

In the late 1800s, it functioned as a service lane to the Fitzroy Arms Hotel and the Australian Coffee Palace.

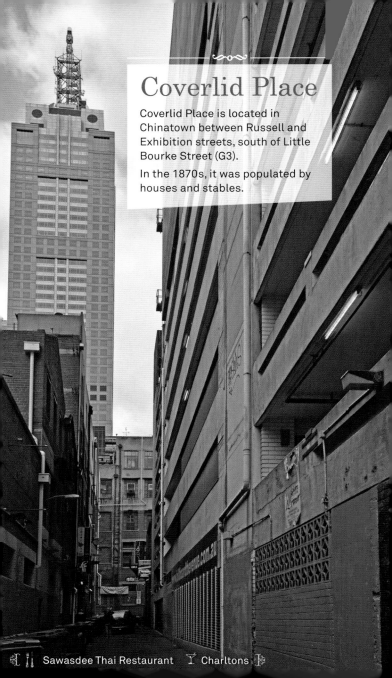

Coverlid Place

Coverlid Place is located in Chinatown between Russell and Exhibition streets, south of Little Bourke Street (G3).

In the 1870s, it was populated by houses and stables.

Sawasdee Thai Restaurant   Charltons

Croft Alley

Croft Alley is located in Chinatown between Russell and Exhibition streets, south of Little Bourke Street, via Paynes Place (G3). The Croft Institute, which is built around a science laboratory, is an iconic bar. An urban legend suggests it was previously a mental hospital.

Street art

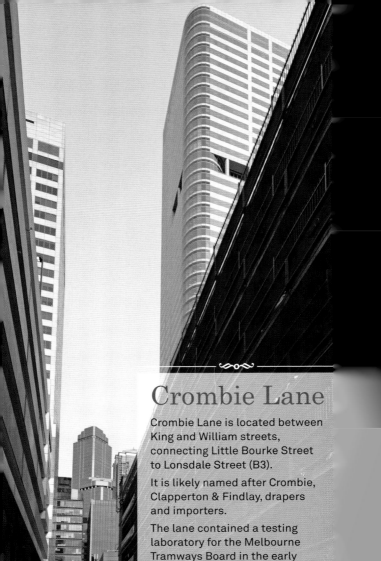

Crombie Lane

Crombie Lane is located between King and William streets, connecting Little Bourke Street to Lonsdale Street (B3).

It is likely named after Crombie, Clapperton & Findlay, drapers and importers.

The lane contained a testing laboratory for the Melbourne Tramways Board in the early 1900s.

Crossley Street

Crossley Street is located between Exhibition and Spring streets, north of Bourke Street (H3). Originally called Romeo Lane, it was designated its current name in 1876 to remove its association with prostitution and disorderly behaviour.

Renowned artist Eugene von Guérard lived in the Von Haus bar in the late 1800s.

De Mille Decorative & Fine Arts, Charles Edward (master shirt maker) and Charles Maimone (tailor) have been situated here for many years.

Becco · Gingerboy · Lucy Folk · Malaya Restaurant

Paella · Pellegrini's Espresso Bar · Traveller · Von Haus

Custom House Lane

Custom House Lane is located between King and William streets, joining Flinders Street to Flinders Lane (B5).

The lane was named in 1876 after the Custom House at 400 Flinders Street, completed in 1859, which is occupied today by the Immigration Museum.

Chinese Fast Food   Hudsons Coffee

Sataybar   SMXL

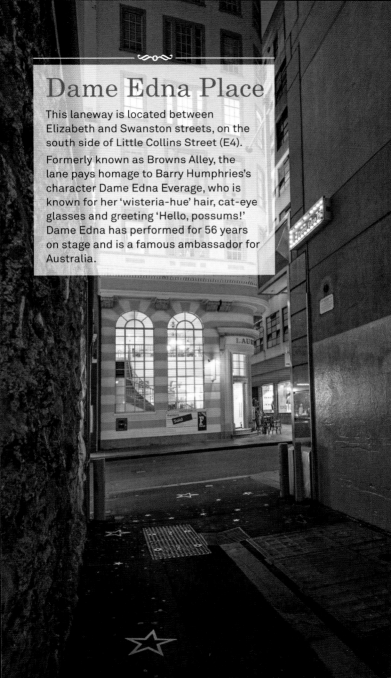

Dame Edna Place

This laneway is located between Elizabeth and Swanston streets, on the south side of Little Collins Street (E4).

Formerly known as Browns Alley, the lane pays homage to Barry Humphries's character Dame Edna Everage, who is known for her 'wisteria-hue' hair, cat-eye glasses and greeting 'Hello, possums!' Dame Edna has performed for 56 years on stage and is a famous ambassador for Australia.

Davisons Place

This residential lane is located between Russell and Exhibition streets, north of Little Lonsdale Street (G2).

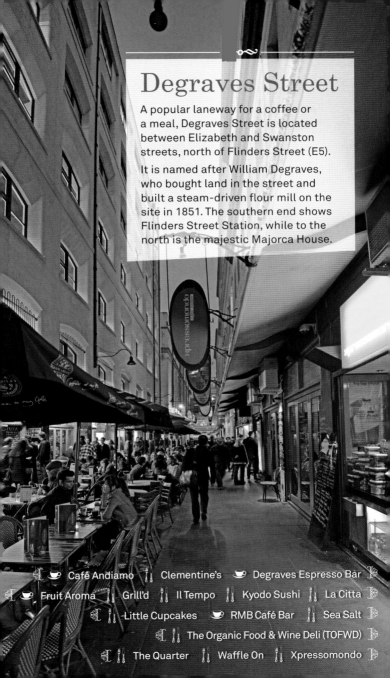

Degraves Street

A popular laneway for a coffee or a meal, Degraves Street is located between Elizabeth and Swanston streets, north of Flinders Street (E5).

It is named after William Degraves, who bought land in the street and built a steam-driven flour mill on the site in 1851. The southern end shows Flinders Street Station, while to the north is the majestic Majorca House.

Café Andiamo Clementine's Degraves Espresso Bar

Fruit Aroma Grill'd Il Tempo Kyodo Sushi La Citta

Little Cupcakes RMB Café Bar Sea Salt

The Organic Food & Wine Deli (TOFWD)

The Quarter Waffle On Xpressomondo

Donaldson Lane

Located between Swanston and Russell streets, Donaldson Lane runs west of Russell Street and north of Little Collins Street (F4).

It was once known as Cyclorama Lane due to its location near the old Cyclorama on Little Collins

Street (now Georges Apartments) and the King's Theatre (now replaced by the Greater Union Cinemas).

Street art is present in the lane.

Cyclorama, located in East Melbourne, of the Battle of Waterloo, Mr. Allan C. Green (1878–1954), 1889. La Trobe Picture Collection, State Library of Victoria.

Cycloramas, 360-degree oil paintings of 122 by 15 metres each, were shown in a circular building. The pictures were lit from above and viewed from a central platform. Real objects such as bushes were merged into the picture. The depression of the 1890s and the arrival of motion pictures caused the demise of cycloramas.

Simpsons Chips & Burgers

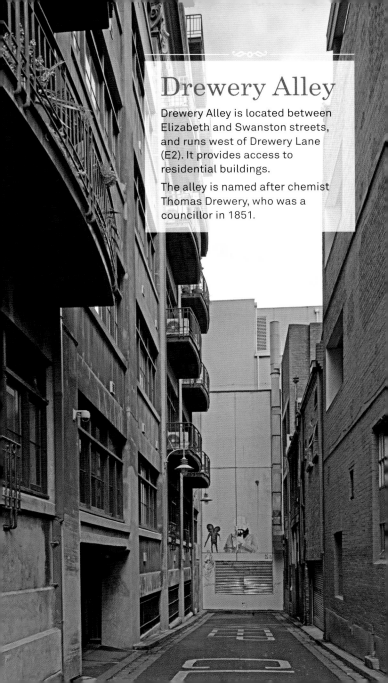

Drewery Alley

Drewery Alley is located between Elizabeth and Swanston streets, and runs west of Drewery Lane (E2). It provides access to residential buildings.

The alley is named after chemist Thomas Drewery, who was a councillor in 1851.

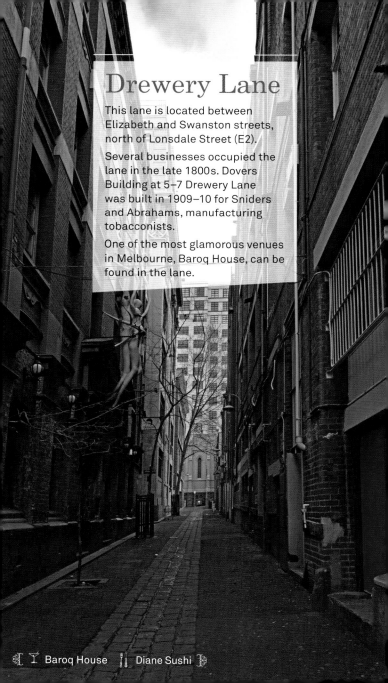

Drewery Lane

This lane is located between Elizabeth and Swanston streets, north of Lonsdale Street (E2).

Several businesses occupied the lane in the late 1800s. Dovers Building at 5–7 Drewery Lane was built in 1909–10 for Sniders and Abrahams, manufacturing tobacconists.

One of the most glamorous venues in Melbourne, Baroq House, can be found in the lane.

Baroq House   Diane Sushi

Drewery Place

Drewery Place is located between Elizabeth and Swanston streets, and runs west of Drewery Lane (E2). It contains heritage warehouses.

Driver Lane

Driver Lane is located between Elizabeth and Swanston streets, north of Little Bourke Street (E3).

It leads into the Strand Arcade and displays murals of postal life and a Penny Black stamp artwork.

The 1890 Money Order Office contains M.O.O. (a tapas dining bar), The Melbourne Shop, Penny Blue Bar and the Melbourne Symphony Orchestra Box Office.

The lane's namesake, Charles Driver (1815–1875), bought land on Elizabeth Street at Melbourne's first crown land sales in 1837.

Duckboard Place

Located between Russell and Exhibition streets, Duckboard Place runs south of Flinders Lane (G5). It is one of Melbourne's street art laneways.

The lane is named after nearby Duckboard House, which was an entertainment centre for soldiers during World War II.

Mary Fortune   Papa Goose   Tonka

Eagle Alley

This alley is located between King and William streets, joining Little Lonsdale Street to La Trobe Street (B2). It was named in 1890.

The northern end enters from behind one of Melbourne's oldest buildings. Further along is a 1920s warehouse and modern buildings.

The shop on the corner was built as a four-room cottage in 1850 by James Heffernan.

Russell's Old Corner Shop Luncheon Room

Electric Place

Electric Place is located between William and Queen streets, connecting A'Beckett Street to Franklin Street (C1).

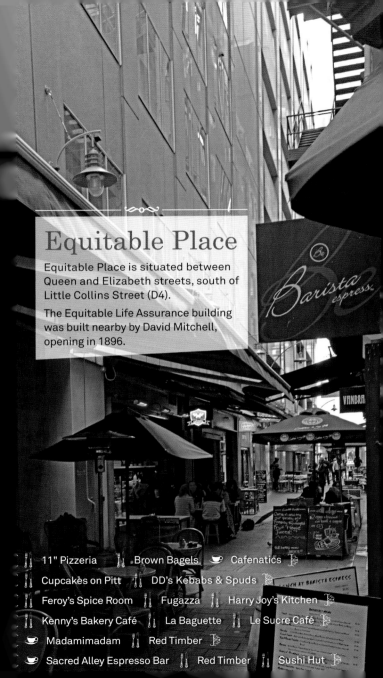

Equitable Place

Equitable Place is situated between Queen and Elizabeth streets, south of Little Collins Street (D4).

The Equitable Life Assurance building was built nearby by David Mitchell, opening in 1896.

11" Pizzeria   Brown Bagels   Cafenatics

Cupcakes on Pitt   DD's Kebabs & Spuds

Feroy's Spice Room   Fugazza   Harry Joy's Kitchen

Kenny's Bakery Café   La Baguette   Le Sucre Café

Madamimadam   Red Timber

Sacred Alley Espresso Bar   Red Timber   Sushi Hut

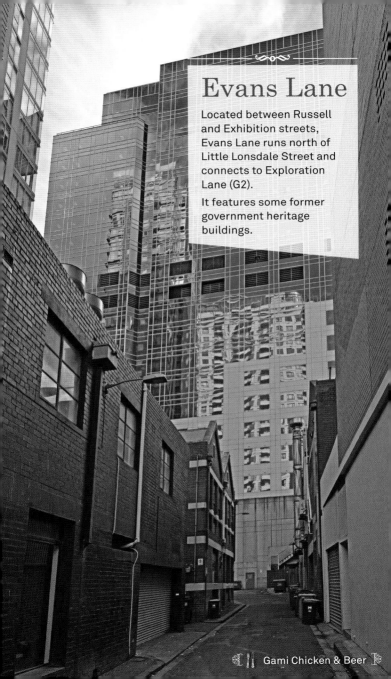

Evans Lane

Located between Russell and Exhibition streets, Evans Lane runs north of Little Lonsdale Street and connects to Exploration Lane (G2).

It features some former government heritage buildings.

Gami Chicken & Beer

Exploration Lane

This lane is located between Russell and Exhibition streets, north of Little Lonsdale Street (G2).

It is named after the Exploration Hotel, formerly on Little Lonsdale Street.

Finlay Alley

Finlay Alley is located between Lonsdale and Little Lonsdale streets, east of Queen Street (D2). It is one of Melbourne's street art laneways.

The alley was named after councillor John Finlay in 1870.

While street art is transitory, there are hidden gems to be discovered.

Flanigan Lane

Flanigan Lane is located between Queen and Elizabeth streets, north of Little Lonsdale Street (D2).

John Flanigan Sr & Jr were the architects who designed Melbourne's Eastern Market. The market was established in 1847 on the corner of Exhibition and Bourke streets.

Street art

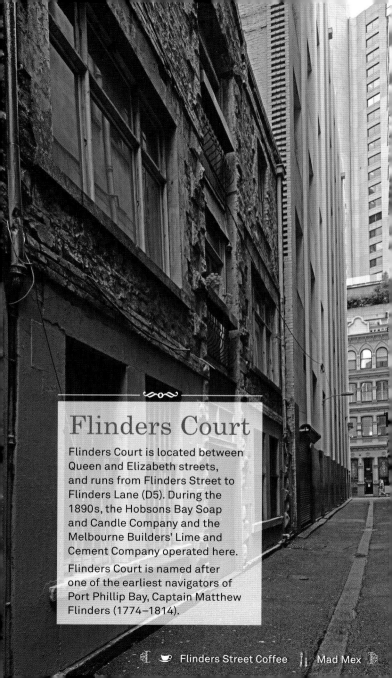

Flinders Court

Flinders Court is located between Queen and Elizabeth streets, and runs from Flinders Street to Flinders Lane (D5). During the 1890s, the Hobsons Bay Soap and Candle Company and the Melbourne Builders' Lime and Cement Company operated here.

Flinders Court is named after one of the earliest navigators of Port Phillip Bay, Captain Matthew Flinders (1774–1814).

Flinders Street Coffee   Mad Mex

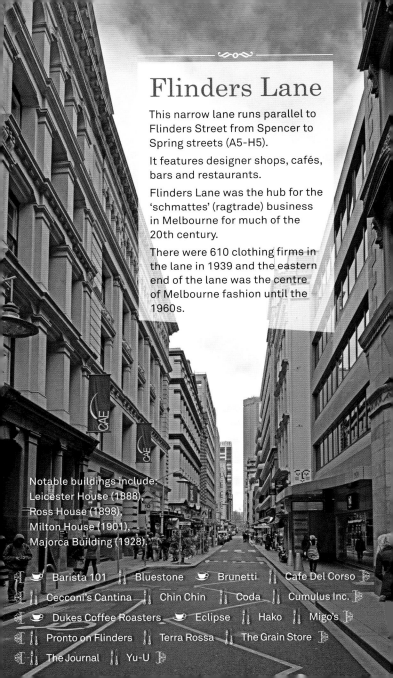

Flinders Lane

This narrow lane runs parallel to Flinders Street from Spencer to Spring streets (A5-H5).

It features designer shops, cafés, bars and restaurants.

Flinders Lane was the hub for the 'schmattes' (ragtrade) business in Melbourne for much of the 20th century.

There were 610 clothing firms in the lane in 1939 and the eastern end of the lane was the centre of Melbourne fashion until the 1960s.

Notable buildings include:
Leicester House (1888),
Ross House (1898),
Milton House (1901),
Majorca Building (1928).

Barista 101   Bluestone   Brunetti   Cafe Del Corso
Cecconi's Cantina   Chin Chin   Coda   Cumulus Inc.
Dukes Coffee Roasters   Eclipse   Hako   Migo's
Pronto on Flinders   Terra Rossa   The Grain Store
The Journal   Yu-U

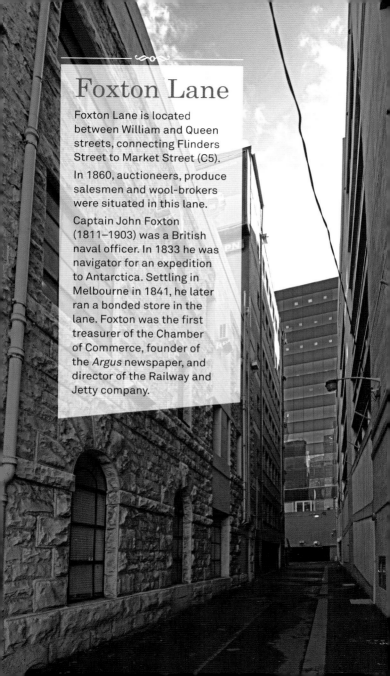

Foxton Lane

Foxton Lane is located between William and Queen streets, connecting Flinders Street to Market Street (C5).

In 1860, auctioneers, produce salesmen and wool-brokers were situated in this lane.

Captain John Foxton (1811–1903) was a British naval officer. In 1833 he was navigator for an expedition to Antarctica. Settling in Melbourne in 1841, he later ran a bonded store in the lane. Foxton was the first treasurer of the Chamber of Commerce, founder of the *Argus* newspaper, and director of the Railway and Jetty company.

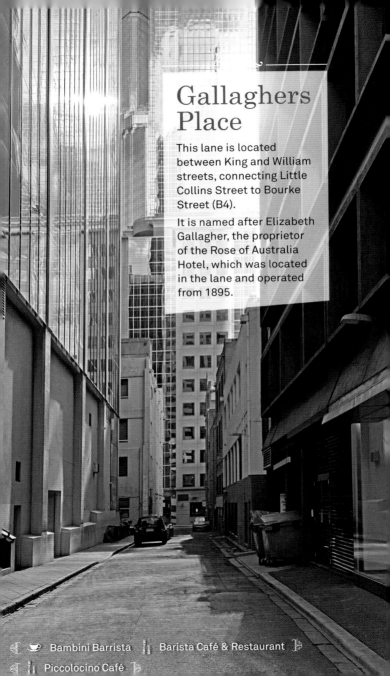

Gallaghers Place

This lane is located between King and William streets, connecting Little Collins Street to Bourke Street (B4).

It is named after Elizabeth Gallagher, the proprietor of the Rose of Australia Hotel, which was located in the lane and operated from 1895.

Bambini Barrista ‖ Barista Café & Restaurant

‖ Piccolocino Café

Geddes Lane

Geddes Lane is located
between King and William
streets, north of Flinders
Lane (B5). It houses several
nightspots.

It is named after William
Geddes (1826–1886), a
machinist whose business
was on Collins Street. He sold
machinery for agriculture and
mining.

George Parade

George Parade is located between Russell and Exhibition streets, connecting Flinders Lane to Collins Street (G5).

It is situated between the Grand Hyatt Melbourne and the 101 Collins building.

The Henry George Club, founded by a group of prominent businessmen in 1918, owned two cottages in the lane.

Gills Alley

Gills Alley is located between Queen and Elizabeth streets, north of Little Collins Street (D4).

In the 1920s, factories and warehouses owned by the Harvey, Shaw and Drake Company were situated here.

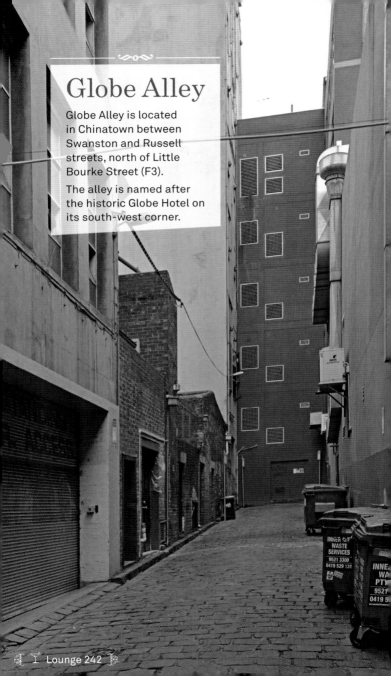

Globe Alley

Globe Alley is located in Chinatown between Swanston and Russell streets, north of Little Bourke Street (F3).

The alley is named after the historic Globe Hotel on its south-west corner.

Godfrey Street

Godfrey Street is located between Spencer and King streets, joining Little Collins Street to Bourke Street (A4).

Two historic buildings visible from the street are the Donkey Wheel House (1891) and the Mail Exchange Hotel (1917).

The Donkey Wheel House, at the north end of the street, was constructed in 1891 for the Melbourne Tramway and Omnibus Company, which developed an extensive cable tram system in 1885.

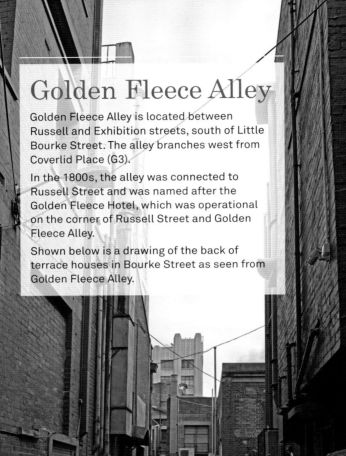

Golden Fleece Alley

Golden Fleece Alley is located between Russell and Exhibition streets, south of Little Bourke Street. The alley branches west from Coverlid Place (G3).

In the 1800s, the alley was connected to Russell Street and was named after the Golden Fleece Hotel, which was operational on the corner of Russell Street and Golden Fleece Alley.

Shown below is a drawing of the back of terrace houses in Bourke Street as seen from Golden Fleece Alley.

Golden Fleece Alley Melbourne E. 1880–1932

Sir William Elliot Johnson (1862–1932)

La Trobe Picture Collection, State Library of Victoria

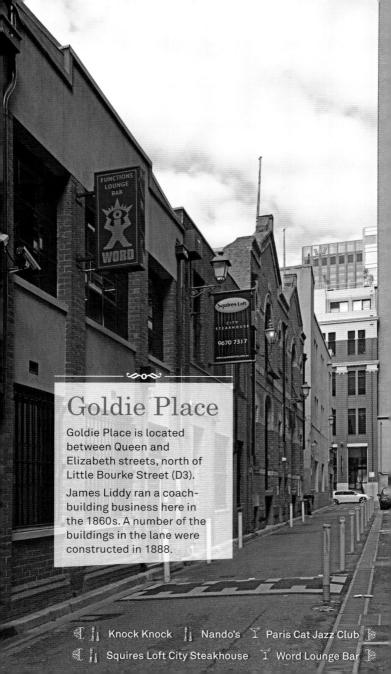

Goldie Place

Goldie Place is located between Queen and Elizabeth streets, north of Little Bourke Street (D3).

James Liddy ran a coach-building business here in the 1860s. A number of the buildings in the lane were constructed in 1888.

Knock Knock   Nando's   Paris Cat Jazz Club

Squires Loft City Steakhouse   Word Lounge Bar

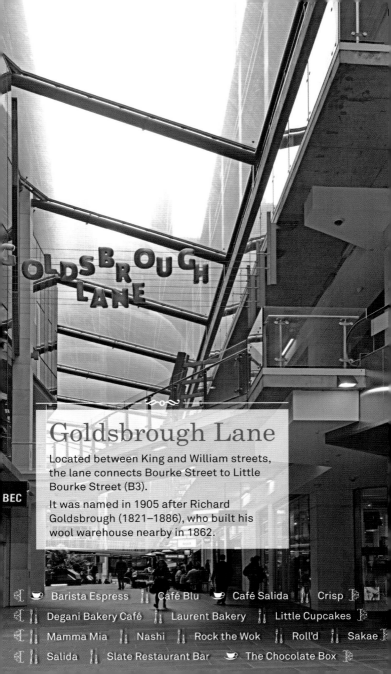

Goldsbrough Lane

Located between King and William streets, the lane connects Bourke Street to Little Bourke Street (B3).

It was named in 1905 after Richard Goldsbrough (1821–1886), who built his wool warehouse nearby in 1862.

Barista Espress | Café Blu | Café Salida | Crisp

Degani Bakery Café | Laurent Bakery | Little Cupcakes

Mamma Mia | Nashi | Rock the Wok | Roll'd | Sakae

Salida | Slate Restaurant Bar | The Chocolate Box

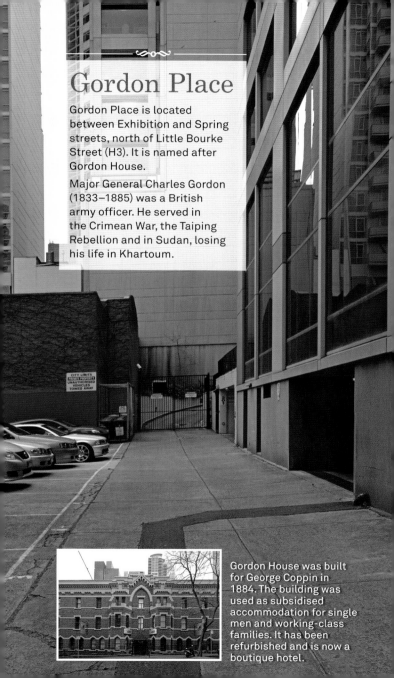

Gordon Place

Gordon Place is located between Exhibition and Spring streets, north of Little Bourke Street (H3). It is named after Gordon House.

Major General Charles Gordon (1833–1885) was a British army officer. He served in the Crimean War, the Taiping Rebellion and in Sudan, losing his life in Khartoum.

Gordon House was built for George Coppin in 1884. The building was used as subsidised accommodation for single men and working-class families. It has been refurbished and is now a boutique hotel.

Gorman Alley

Gorman Alley is located between
Exhibition and Spring streets,
south of Little Lonsdale Street
(H2). The lane connects to
Madame Brussells Lane.

In 1892, the Oddfellows Hotel
could be found on Gorman Alley.

Conference
Centre

Near Gorman Alley
is the remains of a
river red gum tree.
This was one of the
city's last areas to be
cleared of trees.

GPO Lane

This walkway along the Elizabeth Street side of the GPO building (E3) is a popular place for lunch and coffee.

Grice Alley

Grice Alley is located between William and Queen streets, and Bourke and Little Bourke streets (C3), to the west of Little William Street.

Once situated here was Goldsbrough Mort & Co. (1888), an important wool-broking business.

Guests Lane

Guests Lane is located between King and William streets, connecting Little Bourke Street to Lonsdale Street (B3). It divides the Owen Dixon Chambers.

Created around 1915, the lane is named after the T. B. Guest & Co. biscuit factory that was located on the eastern side of the lane from 1866.

Guildford Lane

Guildford Lane is located between Queen and Elizabeth streets, north of Little Lonsdale Street (D2).

The art galleries Screen Space and Utopian Slumps can be found in the lane, which also features a number of historic buildings.

Gurners Lane

Gurners Lane is located between William and Queen streets, and connects Collins Street to Little Collins Street (C4). It is named after Henry Gurner (1819–1883), the Crown Solicitor of Victoria from 1851 to 1880.

The Australian Club (established in 1878) is based at this lane.

🍽 🍴 Don Bay 🍴 Sunny Boy Café 🍴 Terrace Deli 🍴

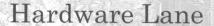

Hardware Lane

The lane is located between Elizabeth and Queen streets, connecting Bourke Street to Lonsdale Street (D3).

It was named after Hardware House (1927) and is located on what was Kirks Bazaar (1840), Melbourne's best-known horse bazaar.

Dynon's Building, a set of four warehouses, has been converted into restaurants and cafés.

- Affogato Espresso Bar
- Aloi Na!
- Amigos
- Aspro Ble
- Basic Bites
- Big Boy BBQ
- Bon à Manger
- Campari House
- Charlie's Bar
- Ciao
- Creperie le Triskel
- Five Boroughs
- Golden Monkey
- Grill Steak Seafood Restaurant
- Kalamaki
- Khokolat Bar
- Larder Section
- Il Nostro Posto
- Max
- Pop Restaurant
- Roll'd
- Sakura
- The Mill
- Triim
- Vons Restaurant & Bar

Hardware Street

Hardware Street is located between Queen and Elizabeth streets, joining Lonsdale Street to Little Lonsdale Street (D2).

Archibalds | Bao Now | Bentoya | Café Miro

CJ Lunch Bar | La La Land | Mini Marche

Pugg Mahones Irish Pub | Silo by Joost | Souperman Café

The Hardware Societe | Unwine | Zambrero

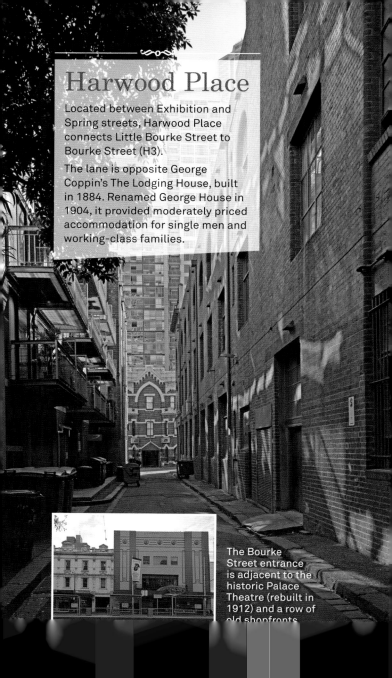

Harwood Place

Located between Exhibition and Spring streets, Harwood Place connects Little Bourke Street to Bourke Street (H3).

The lane is opposite George Coppin's The Lodging House, built in 1884. Renamed George House in 1904, it provided moderately priced accommodation for single men and working-class families.

The Bourke Street entrance is adjacent to the historic Palace Theatre (rebuilt in 1912) and a row of old shopfronts.

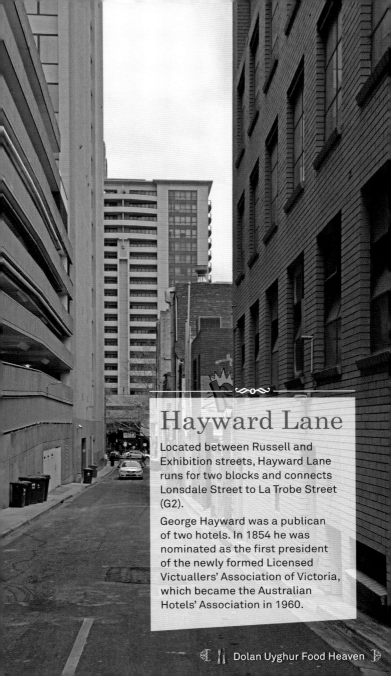

Hayward Lane

Located between Russell and Exhibition streets, Hayward Lane runs for two blocks and connects Lonsdale Street to La Trobe Street (G2).

George Hayward was a publican of two hotels. In 1854 he was nominated as the first president of the newly formed Licensed Victuallers' Association of Victoria, which became the Australian Hotels' Association in 1960.

Dolan Uyghur Food Heaven

Healeys Lane

Healeys Lane is located
between King and William
streets, south of Little Lonsdale
Street (B2). In the 1890s, the
lane was used by a timber yard
and ironworks.

1st Salt & Pepper   Bluebag   Cilantro Star   Donahue's
Gami   Healthy Az   In A Rush   Kenny's Bakery Café
le trai teur   Little Café on Healeys Lane   Mapo Grill & Bar
Mr. Nice Guy   Shinssi Hwaro   Shuji Sushi

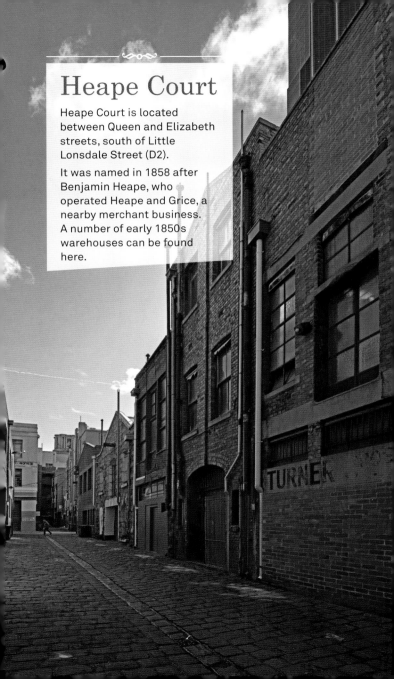

Heape Court

Heape Court is located between Queen and Elizabeth streets, south of Little Lonsdale Street (D2).

It was named in 1858 after Benjamin Heape, who operated Heape and Grice, a nearby merchant business. A number of early 1850s warehouses can be found here.

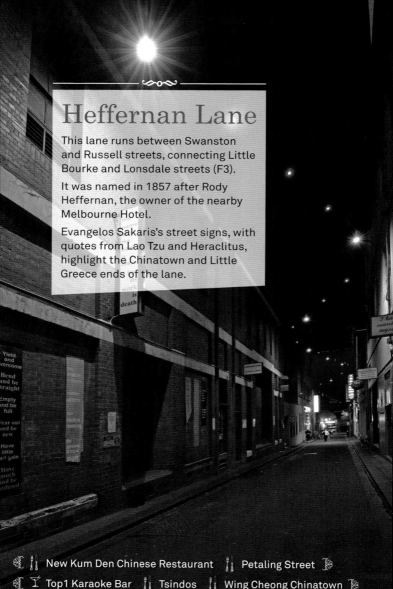

Heffernan Lane

This lane runs between Swanston and Russell streets, connecting Little Bourke and Lonsdale streets (F3).

It was named in 1857 after Rody Heffernan, the owner of the nearby Melbourne Hotel.

Evangelos Sakaris's street signs, with quotes from Lao Tzu and Heraclitus, highlight the Chinatown and Little Greece ends of the lane.

New Kum Den Chinese Restaurant   Petaling Street

Top1 Karaoke Bar   Tsindos   Wing Cheong Chinatown

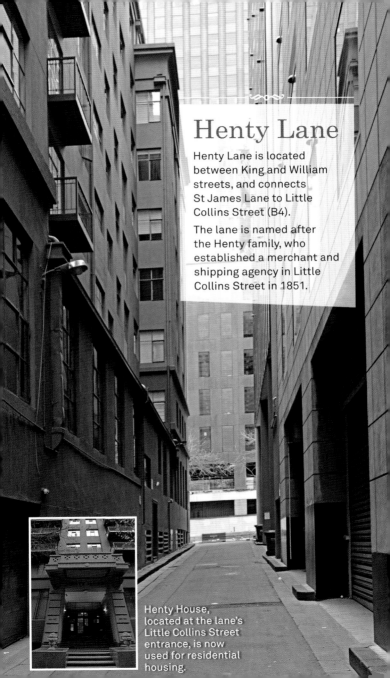

Henty Lane

Henty Lane is located between King and William streets, and connects St James Lane to Little Collins Street (B4).

The lane is named after the Henty family, who established a merchant and shipping agency in Little Collins Street in 1851.

Henty House, located at the lane's Little Collins Street entrance, is now used for residential housing.

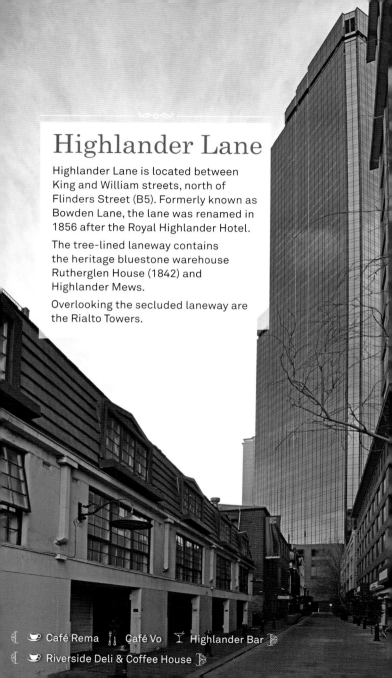

Highlander Lane

Highlander Lane is located between King and William streets, north of Flinders Street (B5). Formerly known as Bowden Lane, the lane was renamed in 1856 after the Royal Highlander Hotel.

The tree-lined laneway contains the heritage bluestone warehouse Rutherglen House (1842) and Highlander Mews.

Overlooking the secluded laneway are the Rialto Towers.

☕ Café Rema   🍴 Café Vo   🍸 Highlander Bar

☕ Riverside Deli & Coffee House

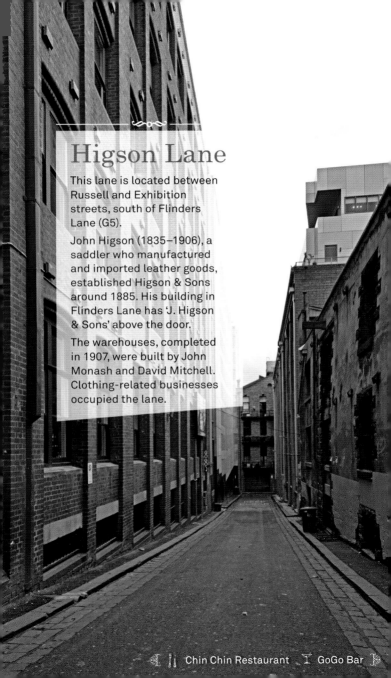

Higson Lane

This lane is located between Russell and Exhibition streets, south of Flinders Lane (G5).

John Higson (1835–1906), a saddler who manufactured and imported leather goods, established Higson & Sons around 1885. His building in Flinders Lane has 'J. Higson & Sons' above the door.

The warehouses, completed in 1907, were built by John Monash and David Mitchell. Clothing-related businesses occupied the lane.

Chin Chin Restaurant   GoGo Bar

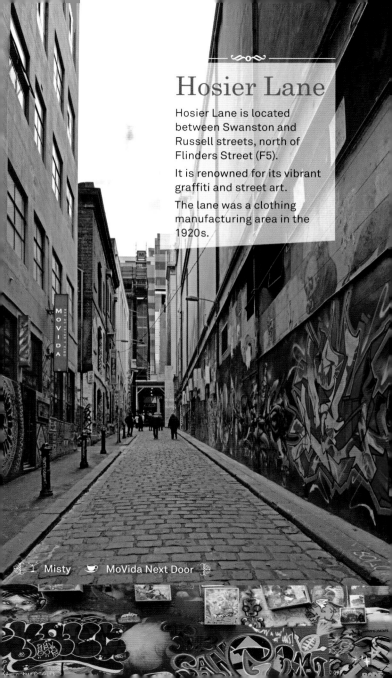

Hosier Lane

Hosier Lane is located between Swanston and Russell streets, north of Flinders Street (F5).

It is renowned for its vibrant graffiti and street art.

The lane was a clothing manufacturing area in the 1920s.

Misty   MoVida Next Door

Heath Ledger as The Joker, painted by Owen Ditte.

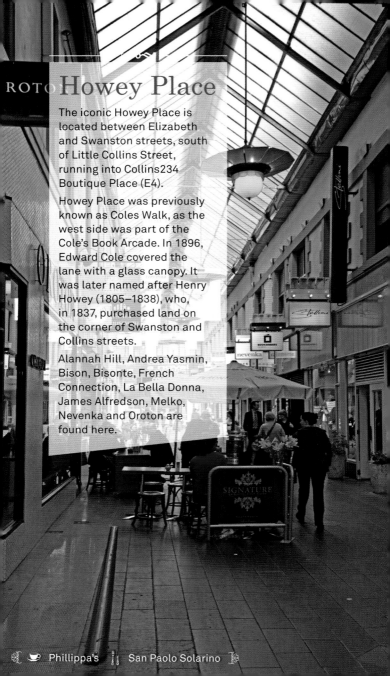

Howey Place

The iconic Howey Place is located between Elizabeth and Swanston streets, south of Little Collins Street, running into Collins234 Boutique Place (E4).

Howey Place was previously known as Coles Walk, as the west side was part of the Cole's Book Arcade. In 1896, Edward Cole covered the lane with a glass canopy. It was later named after Henry Howey (1805–1838), who, in 1837, purchased land on the corner of Swanston and Collins streets.

Alannah Hill, Andrea Yasmin, Bison, Bisonte, French Connection, La Bella Donna, James Alfredson, Melko, Nevenka and Oroton are found here.

Phillippa's   San Paolo Solarino

Howitt Lane

Howitt Lane is located between Exhibition and Spring streets, north of Flinders Lane (H5).

Originally called Booth Lane, in 1905 the name was changed to Howitt Lane after Dr Godfrey Howitt, who, in the 1840s, had a cottage and garden from Collins Street to Flinders Lane along Spring Street.

Howitt was one of the first doctors at the Royal Melbourne Hospital, founding vice-president of the Royal Society of Victoria and council member of the University of Melbourne.

Hub Arcade

The arcade connects to Little Collins Street and the Royal Arcade, near Elizabeth Street (E4).

Chokolait · de Alleyway · Gourmet Curry Hut

I Love Mes Cheveux · Mackerel Sushi · Phở 102 Saigon

Hughs Alley

The short alley is located in Chinatown, between Swanston and Russell streets, south of Little Bourke Street (F3).

四邑大樓

Boss Karaoke · Chi Lounge · Westlake Restaurant

Jane Bell Lane

This lane is part of the Queen Victoria Melbourne (QV) complex. It is located between Swanston and Russell streets, and Lonsdale and Little Lonsdale streets (F2).

Jane Bell (1873–1959) was the matron of the Royal Melbourne Hospital from 1910 to 1934. She introduced many innovations to Victoria's nursing techniques.

The Bean Room

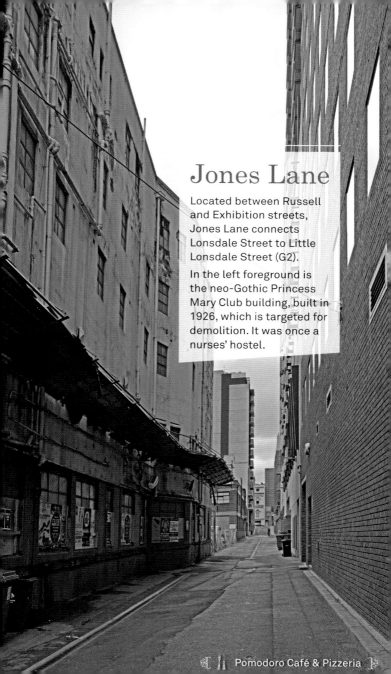

Jones Lane

Located between Russell and Exhibition streets, Jones Lane connects Lonsdale Street to Little Lonsdale Street (G2).

In the left foreground is the neo-Gothic Princess Mary Club building, built in 1926, which is targeted for demolition. It was once a nurses' hostel.

Pomodoro Café & Pizzeria

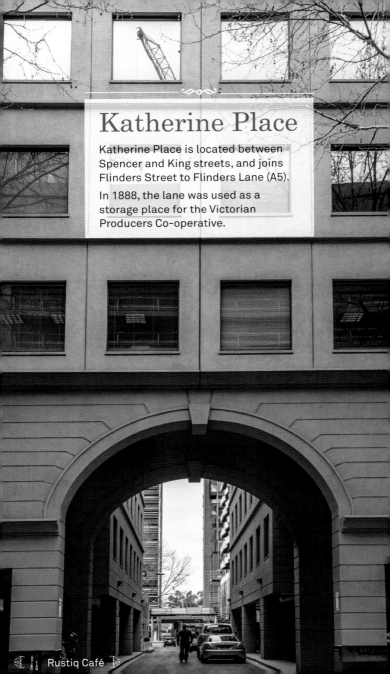

Katherine Place

Katherine Place is located between Spencer and King streets, and joins Flinders Street to Flinders Lane (A5).

In 1888, the lane was used as a storage place for the Victorian Producers Co-operative.

Rustiq Café

Knox Lane

This lane is located between Elizabeth and Swanston streets, north of Little Lonsdale Street (E2).

Previously known as Partner Alley, it was renamed in 1896 after the adjacent John Knox Church (now Church of Christ) on Swanston Street.

Don Don

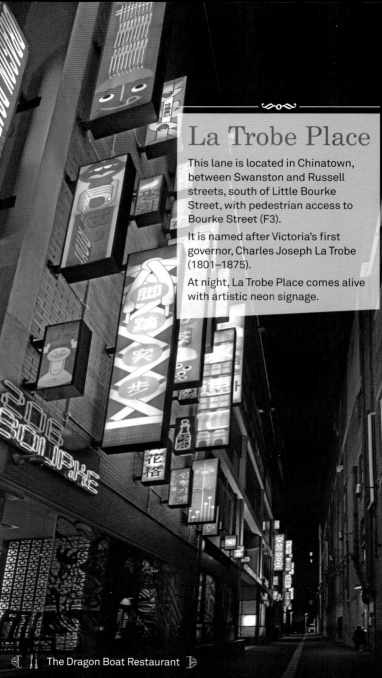

La Trobe Place

This lane is located in Chinatown, between Swanston and Russell streets, south of Little Bourke Street, with pedestrian access to Bourke Street (F3).

It is named after Victoria's first governor, Charles Joseph La Trobe (1801–1875).

At night, La Trobe Place comes alive with artistic neon signage.

The Dragon Boat Restaurant

Lacey Place

Lacey Place is located between Russell and Exhibition streets, north of Little Bourke Street (G3).

In 1870, Patrick Lacey occupied a house in the lane.

The Lion Garden is situated in the lane. It is part of Ancient Times House, used as Urban Seed's The Den.

Empress of China | Golden Orchids

Langs Lane

Langs Lane is located between Spencer and King streets, connecting Bourke Street to Little Bourke Street (A3).

The narrow walkway at the southern end of the lane lies between the Eliza Tinsley building (1905) and the Alto Hotel (1916). The lane was featured in the movie *Malcolm*.

Lees Place

This nondescript lane is located between Russell and Exhibition streets, connecting Little Bourke Street to Exhibition Street (G3).

Her Majesty's Theatre can be seen at the northern end of the lane.

Benjamin Lee (1820–1899) was an ironmonger who established a store in Bourke Street around 1850. Melbourne's first hansom cab was built by Lee, John Pascoe Fawkner and Edward Duckett.

Lee Served on the Melbourne City Council for over 20 years.

Her Majesty's Theatre opened in 1886, when it was named The Alexandra and, later, The Princess of Wales. In 1900, the theatre was refurbished and given its current name. Dame Nellie Melba made her Australian opera debut at the theatre in 1911.

Chine on Paramount | Golden Delicious

Nihonbashi Zen | The Elephant and Wheelbarrow

Liberty Lane

The popular Liberty Lane is located between Spencer and King streets, and connects Collins Street to Francis Street (A4).

perkup espresso bar

Open 365 Days
Mon to Fri 5.30am to 9pm
Weekends 6.30am to late

great coffee guaranteed

Chick-In Choix Creperie Café JT's Fine Catering
Minx Coffee Bar Pallet Espresso Perkup Expresso Bar
Purple Peanuts Japanese Café Wonderful Garden

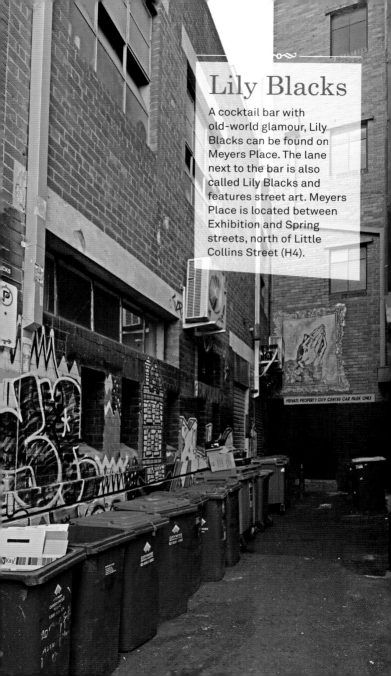

Lily Blacks

A cocktail bar with old-world glamour, Lily Blacks can be found on Meyers Place. The lane next to the bar is also called Lily Blacks and features street art. Meyers Place is located between Exhibition and Spring streets, north of Little Collins Street (H4).

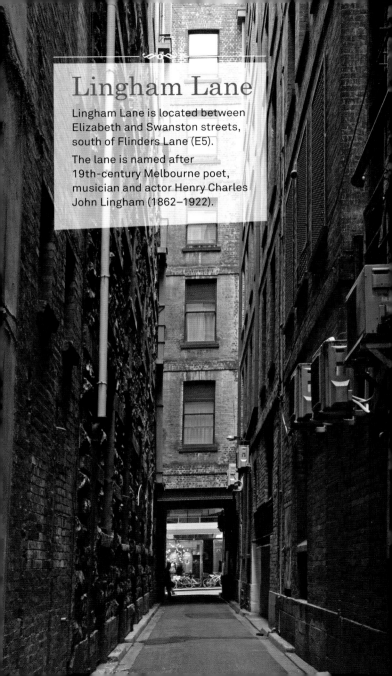

Lingham Lane

Lingham Lane is located between
Elizabeth and Swanston streets,
south of Flinders Lane (E5).

The lane is named after
19th-century Melbourne poet,
musician and actor Henry Charles
John Lingham (1862–1922).

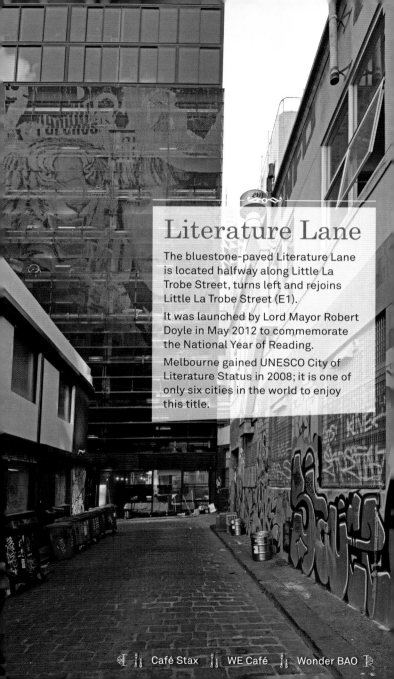

Literature Lane

The bluestone-paved Literature Lane is located halfway along Little La Trobe Street, turns left and rejoins Little La Trobe Street (E1).

It was launched by Lord Mayor Robert Doyle in May 2012 to commemorate the National Year of Reading.

Melbourne gained UNESCO City of Literature Status in 2008; it is one of only six cities in the world to enjoy this title.

Café Stax   WE Café   Wonder BAO

Little Bourke Street

This street runs from Spencer Street in the west to Spring Street in the east (A3–H3).

Grand arches mark Chinatown as it extends from Swanston Street to Spring Street. The theatre district is at the eastern end, with the elegant buildings of Her Majesty's Theatre, the Comedy Theatre and the Princess Theatre in close proximity.

Little Bourke Street is named after Sir Richard Bourke, Governor of New South Wales from 1831 to 1837. He named Melbourne in 1837 after British Prime Minister William Lamb, the 2nd Viscount Melbourne. His wife, Caroline Lamb, became famous for her love affair with English poet Lord Byron.

There are almost 100 restaurants situated in this street. Pictured is the entrance to Chinatown on Spring Street (H3).

墨爾本

唐人街

+39 pizzeria | Bamboo House Restaurant

Brother Baba Budan | City BBQ | Crystal Jade

Dragon Boat | Empress of China | Golden Orchids | Kuni's

Lemon Bistro | Longrain Melbourne | Mezzo

Mrs Parma's | Shanghai Street Dumpling | Shark Fin Inn

Shou Sumiyaki | The Apartment Restaurant

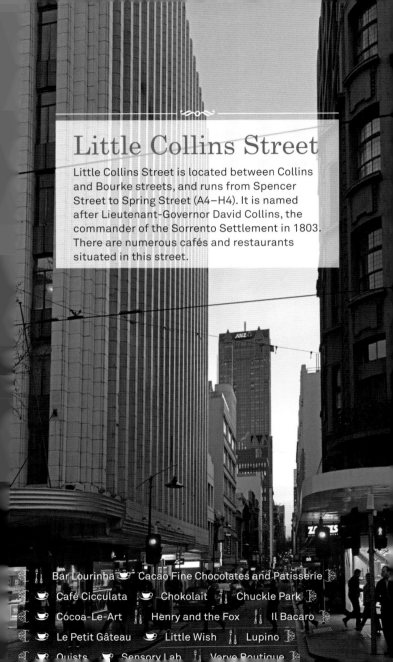

Little Collins Street

Little Collins Street is located between Collins and Bourke streets, and runs from Spencer Street to Spring Street (A4–H4). It is named after Lieutenant-Governor David Collins, the commander of the Sorrento Settlement in 1803. There are numerous cafés and restaurants situated in this street.

Bar Lourinha Cacao Fine Chocolates and Patisserie
Café Cicculata Chokolait Chuckle Park
Cocoa-Le-Art Henry and the Fox Il Bacaro
Le Petit Gâteau Little Wish Lupino
Quists Sensory Lab Verve Boutique

Little La Trobe Street

This street is located between La Trobe and A'Beckett streets, east of Elizabeth Street (E1). It is named after Charles Joseph La Trobe, the first Governor of Victoria (1851–1854).

La Trobe Street was constructed around 1850, and in 1857 it was occupied by plumbers, food merchants, clothing businesses and blacksmiths.

Art can be seen along the street.

A Little Bird Told Me ☕ Café Stax ☕ Gloria Jean's Coffees

☕ Pearson & Murphy's Café 🍴 Spice Up

Little Lonsdale Street

Little Lonsdale Street is located between La Trobe and Lonsdale streets (A2–H2).

It is named after Captain William Lonsdale (1799–1864), who supervised the founding of Melbourne.

In the 1800s, the street between Exhibition and Spring streets was known as 'Little Lon', a red-light district. It began as a working-class area, with furniture, engineering and small shops established there later.

1000£Bend   Back Pocket Café   Café 18
Café 111   City Grill Room   Corean House
Déjà Vu Bar and Lounge   Don Too   Five 2 Five
Gami   Giraffe Café   JWOW Wine Bar   Little Peninsula
Rue Bebélons   Shalom Indonesia   Shop 7
The Moat   The Workers' Food Room   Troika Bar

Little Queen Street

Little Queen Street is located between William and Queen streets, and connects Bourke Street to Little Bourke Street (C3).

It is named after Queen Adelaide, wife of King William IV.

The view north shows the Old High Court Building. The street was formerly known as Synagogue Lane, since it was home to Melbourne's first synagogue (established in 1847 and rebuilt in 1855).

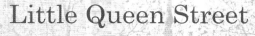

CBD Bakery   Donato's Licensed Café Restaurant

Little William Street

Little William Street is located between Bourke and Little Bourke Street, east of William Street (C3). It is named after King William IV. The domed building visible is the Supreme Court of Victoria.

Liverpool Street

Liverpool Street is located between Exhibition and Spring streets, north of Bourke Street (H3).

The street, once a red-light district, was originally named Juliet Terrace.

Bamboo House   Double Happiness Bar

Horoki Casual Dining Bar   Laksa Me   Little Malaysia

New Gold Mountain   Saigon Inn

Sake Bar   Shimbashi Soba

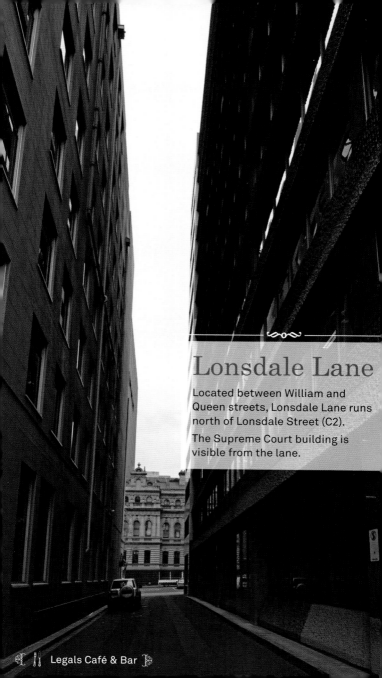

Lonsdale Lane

Located between William and Queen streets, Lonsdale Lane runs north of Lonsdale Street (C2).

The Supreme Court building is visible from the lane.

Legals Café & Bar

Louden Place

Louden Place is located between Elizabeth and Swanston streets, south of Little Bourke Street (E3).

William Louden, a grocer, arrived in Melbourne in 1847 and operated a store on Swanston Street.

The Swanston Hotel, Grand Mercure

Crown Café Bakery   Louden Kitchen & Grill   Yoyogi

Macs Lane

The lane adjacent to Macs Hotel is located between Elizabeth and Swanston streets, north of Franklin Street (E0).

Buildings around the hotel in the 1850s, included stables for 100 horses, accommodation for the gold escort, sheds and a lock-up.

Macs Hotel is the last surviving coaching inn in Melbourne's CBD.

Macs Hotel was built in 1853 from bluestone and bricks. It operated as a hotel and coach terminal during the Ballarat goldrush. John McMillan was the hotel's licencee.

Macs Hotel

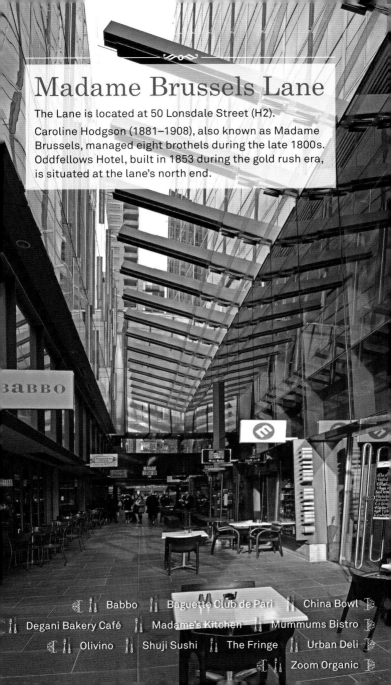

Madame Brussels Lane

The Lane is located at 50 Lonsdale Street (H2).

Caroline Hodgson (1881–1908), also known as Madame Brussels, managed eight brothels during the late 1800s. Oddfellows Hotel, built in 1853 during the gold rush era, is situated at the lane's north end.

Babbo | Baguette Club de Pari | China Bowl
Degani Bakery Café | Madame's Kitchen | Mummums Bistro
Olivino | Shuji Sushi | The Fringe | Urban Deli
Zoom Organic

Malthouse Lane

The lane is located between Russell and Exhibition streets, south of Flinders Lane (G5).

Around 1869, Samuel Burston owned a five-storey steam and gas-powered malthouse. Burston successfully introduced the Saladin process for making malt and exported malt to all the colonies.

Terra Rossa ⫶ The French Brasserie ⫶ Wagamama

Manchester Lane

Manchester Lane is located between Elizabeth and Swanston streets, joining Flinders Lane to Collins Street (E5).

It bypasses Manchester House (1915), one of Melbourne's great fashion buildings. The lane once included many fabric warehouses.

Fashion shops are situated here.

Maccaroni Trattoria Italiana | Manchester Lane | Shebeen

Manchester Unity Arcade

The arcade is located on the corner of Swanston and Collins streets (E4). It leads to the Manchester Unity building, which was constructed in 1932 and modelled on the 1927 Chicago Tribune Tower. It was the first building in Victoria to have escalators, the tallest in Melbourne at the time, and was completed in 11 months due to workers working around-the-clock shifts.

The arcade features designs sand-blasted on a series of black marble tablets, polished brass and copper, and an elaborate mosaic floor.

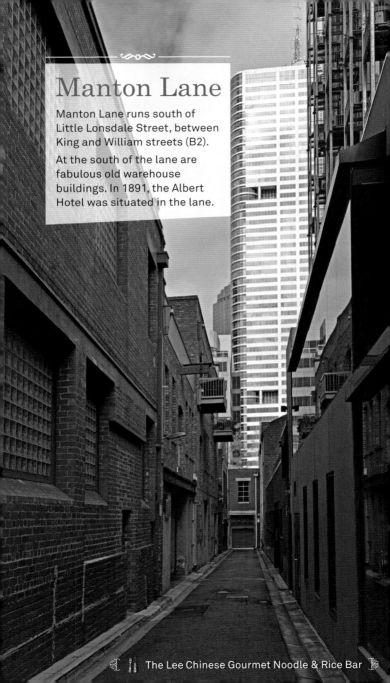

Manton Lane

Manton Lane runs south of Little Lonsdale Street, between King and William streets (B2).

At the south of the lane are fabulous old warehouse buildings. In 1891, the Albert Hotel was situated in the lane.

The Lee Chinese Gourmet Noodle & Rice Bar

Market Lane

Located in Chinatown between Russell and Exhibition streets, the lane runs from Bourke to Little Bourke streets (G3).

The paving displays the Chinese symbol for longevity and the entrance has Chinese dragons.

The Eastern Market was established in 1847 at the corner of Exhibition and Bourke streets and gave the lane its name. The market's role of supplying fresh produce to Melbourne was taken over by the Queen Victoria Market in 1878.

Ding Dong Lounge   Fireflies Club   Flower Drum

Hofbräuhaus   Hu Tong Dumpling Bar   iHotPot

Japanese Noodle Café   Shoya   Welcome Stranger

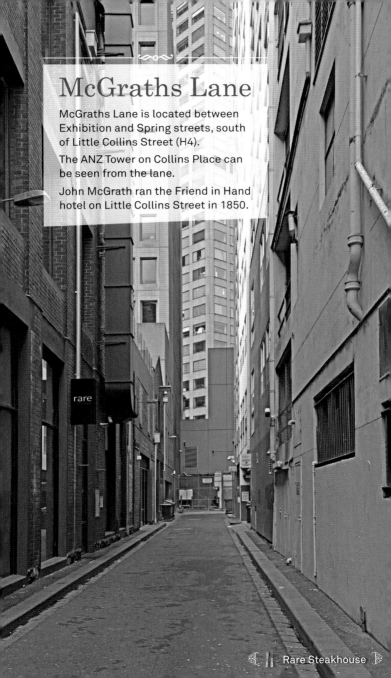

McGraths Lane

McGraths Lane is located between Exhibition and Spring streets, south of Little Collins Street (H4).

The ANZ Tower on Collins Place can be seen from the lane.

John McGrath ran the Friend in Hand hotel on Little Collins Street in 1850.

Rare Steakhouse

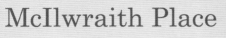

McIlwraith Place

McIlwraith Place connects Little Collins and Bourke streets, and lies between Exhibition and Spring streets (H4).

The lane leads through the Parkade Car Park, past the historic Mitty's Newsagency and Neon Parc Art Gallery.

It is named after John McIlwraith, who was Lord Mayor of Melbourne from 1873 to 1874.

Club Asuka

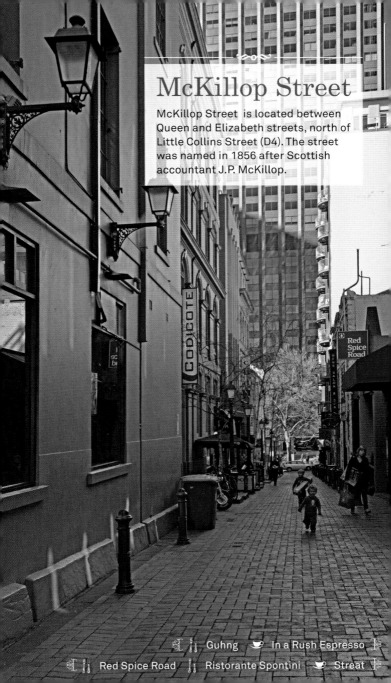

McKillop Street

McKillop Street is located between Queen and Elizabeth streets, north of Little Collins Street (D4). The street was named in 1856 after Scottish accountant J.P. McKillop.

Guhng ☕ In a Rush Espresso

Red Spice Road ｜｜ Ristorante Spontini ☕ Streat

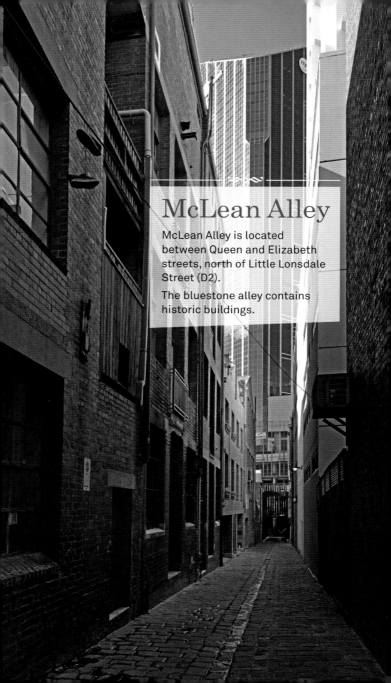

McLean Alley

McLean Alley is located between Queen and Elizabeth streets, north of Little Lonsdale Street (D2).

The bluestone alley contains historic buildings.

Melbourne Place

This laneway, is located off Russell Street, between Bourke and Little Collins streets (G4). It has been in use since 1839.

The Kelvin Club, located here, was founded in 1927 and is a private members' club named after Scottish physicist Lord Kelvin (1824–1907).

Menzies Alley

Menzies Alley is located in the Melbourne Central precinct. It leads from Elizabeth Street and Little Lonsdale Street into Menzies Place (E2).

Ajisen Ramen   Café Era   Chilli India
Cupcake Bakery   Food Inc.   Max Brenner Chocolate Bar
Oriental Teahouse   Spiga

Merlin Alley

Merlin Alley is located between William and Queen streets, south of Little Bourke Street (C3).

In the 1860s the alley contained a clothes cleaner, gunsmith and machinist.

Chi Kitchen

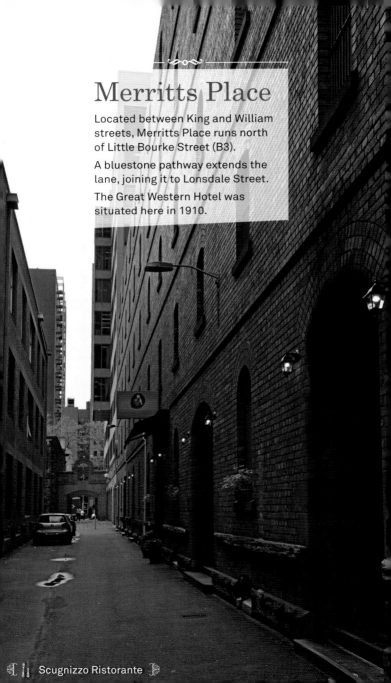

Merritts Place

Located between King and William streets, Merritts Place runs north of Little Bourke Street (B3).

A bluestone pathway extends the lane, joining it to Lonsdale Street.

The Great Western Hotel was situated here in 1910.

Scugnizzo Ristorante

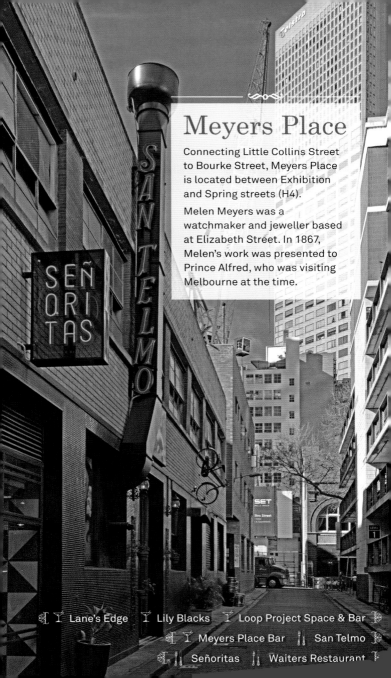

Meyers Place

Connecting Little Collins Street to Bourke Street, Meyers Place is located between Exhibition and Spring streets (H4).

Melen Meyers was a watchmaker and jeweller based at Elizabeth Street. In 1867, Melen's work was presented to Prince Alfred, who was visiting Melbourne at the time.

Lane's Edge   Lily Blacks   Loop Project Space & Bar

Meyers Place Bar   San Telmo

Señoritas   Waiters Restaurant

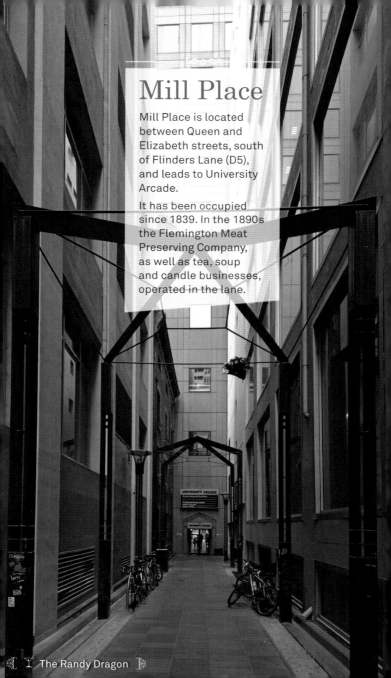

Mill Place

Mill Place is located between Queen and Elizabeth streets, south of Flinders Lane (D5), and leads to University Arcade.

It has been occupied since 1839. In the 1890s the Flemington Meat Preserving Company, as well as tea, soup and candle businesses, operated in the lane.

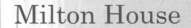

Milton House

This narrow laneway is located between Exhibition and Spring streets and runs from Flinders Street to Flinders Lane (H5).

It emerges at Milton House and has multiple rows of steps.

Milton House was built in 1901 as a private hospital. The facade is a rare example of Art Nouveau design.

Mitre Lane

Located between William and Queen streets, and Collins and Little Collins streets, Mitre Lane runs west of Bank Place (C4).

The lane divides the historic buildings of the Mitre Tavern (1867) and Bank House.

Mitre Tavern

Moylans Lane

Moylans Lane is located between Market and Queen streets, north of Flinders Lane (C5).

Carpenters and a sign-writer lived in the lane in the late 1880s.

Tonic House

New Chancery Lane

New Chancery Lane is located between William and Queen streets, and connects Little Collins Street to Bourke Street (C4).

The view south shows the magnificent Temple Court building.

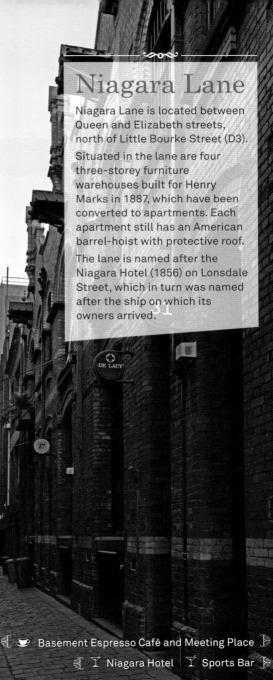

Niagara Lane

Niagara Lane is located between Queen and Elizabeth streets, north of Little Bourke Street (D3).

Situated in the lane are four three-storey furniture warehouses built for Henry Marks in 1887, which have been converted to apartments. Each apartment still has an American barrel-hoist with protective roof.

The lane is named after the Niagara Hotel (1856) on Lonsdale Street, which in turn was named after the ship on which its owners arrived.

Basement Espresso Café and Meeting Place

Niagara Hotel   Sports Bar

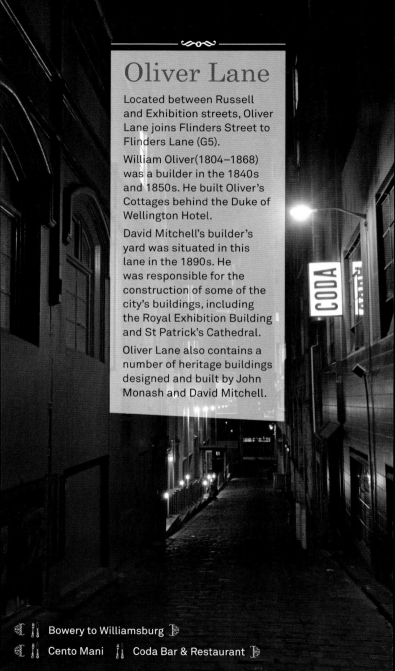

Oliver Lane

Located between Russell and Exhibition streets, Oliver Lane joins Flinders Street to Flinders Lane (G5).

William Oliver(1804–1868) was a builder in the 1840s and 1850s. He built Oliver's Cottages behind the Duke of Wellington Hotel.

David Mitchell's builder's yard was situated in this lane in the 1890s. He was responsible for the construction of some of the city's buildings, including the Royal Exhibition Building and St Patrick's Cathedral.

Oliver Lane also contains a number of heritage buildings designed and built by John Monash and David Mitchell.

Bowery to Williamsburg

Cento Mani   Coda Bar & Restaurant

Ozimek Lane

This lane is located between Queen and Elizabeth streets, and Lonsdale and Little Lonsdale streets, running west of Hardware Street (D2).

Street art can be found here.

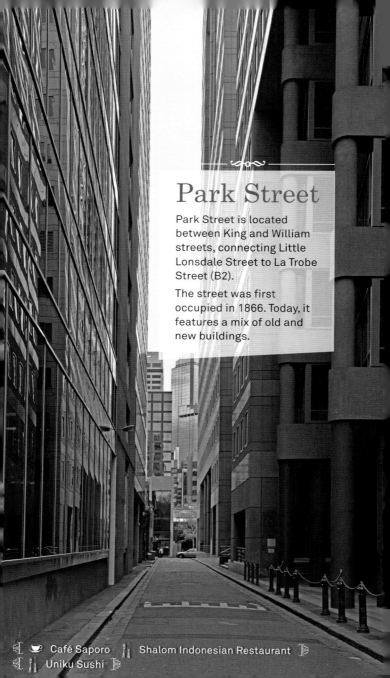

Park Street

Park Street is located between King and William streets, connecting Little Lonsdale Street to La Trobe Street (B2).

The street was first occupied in 1866. Today, it features a mix of old and new buildings.

Café Saporo | Shalom Indonesian Restaurant

Uniku Sushi

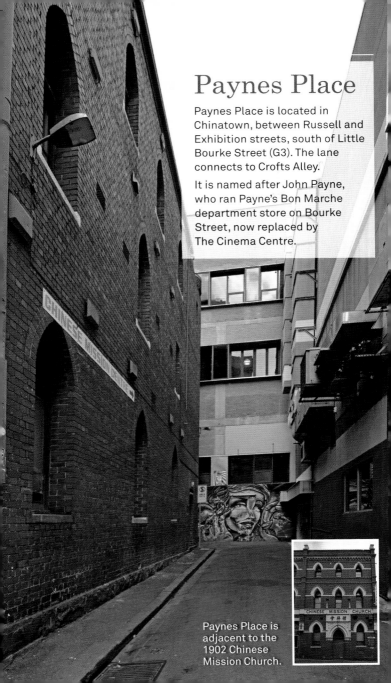

Paynes Place

Paynes Place is located in Chinatown, between Russell and Exhibition streets, south of Little Bourke Street (G3). The lane connects to Crofts Alley.

It is named after John Payne, who ran Payne's Bon Marche department store on Bourke Street, now replaced by The Cinema Centre.

Paynes Place is adjacent to the 1902 Chinese Mission Church.

Pender Place

Located between Russell and Exhibition streets, Pender Place leads north from Little Bourke Street (G3).

William Pender built the schooner *Enterprize* in Hobart in 1829. *Enterprize* was purchased by John Pascoe Fawkner (1798–1869) and carried a settlement party to the future site of Melbourne in 1835.

Golden Orchids Malaysian Restaurant   ☕ Pink Café

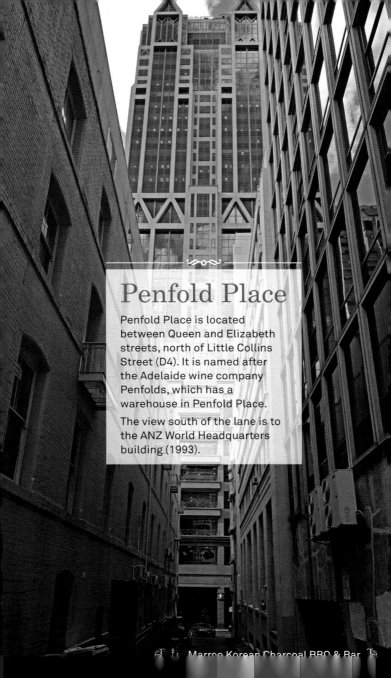

Penfold Place

Penfold Place is located between Queen and Elizabeth streets, north of Little Collins Street (D4). It is named after the Adelaide wine company Penfolds, which has a warehouse in Penfold Place.

The view south of the lane is to the ANZ World Headquarters building (1993).

Marroo Korean Charcoal BBQ & Bar

Phoenix Lane

Phoenix Lane is located opposite the Flagstaff Gardens, between La Trobe and Jeffcott streets, west of King Street (A1).

The bluestone houses in and around this residential lane were built from 1863 to 1870.

The Fenwick Brothers, clothing manufacturers and importers from London, owned the site from the 1850s. In the 1870s they established the Phoenix Clothing Company, which operated from the 1854 three-storey shop in the lane.

Biryani House   King's Café Phoenix

Pink Alley

Located between Russell and Exhibition streets, Pink Alley runs south of Little Collins Street (G4).

Port Phillip Arcade

Port Phillip Arcade is located between
Elizabeth and Swanston streets, and
connects Flinders Street to Flinders Lane
via Scott Alley (E5).

Alice Nivens   Cake Deco   Jolly J's

Kim Sing   Ratee Thai   Sushi Ten

Portland Lane

Portland Lane is located between Swanston and Russell streets, connecting Little Collins Street to Russell Street (F4).

The Portland Lane Café and the historic Portland Hotel (1889) are adjacent to Portland Lane.

The James Squire Brewhouse displays the history of Australia's first brewer.

James Squire Brewhouse   Portland Hotel

Portland Lane Café

Postal Lane

This lane runs north from Bourke Street to Little Bourke Street at the east end of the GPO building (E3). It is a popular eating place.

CA de VIN   Kenzan   Ramen Ya

Premiers Lane

Premiers Lane connects Treasury Place to St Andrews Place (I4).

The lane lies adjacent to the Victorian State Government offices.

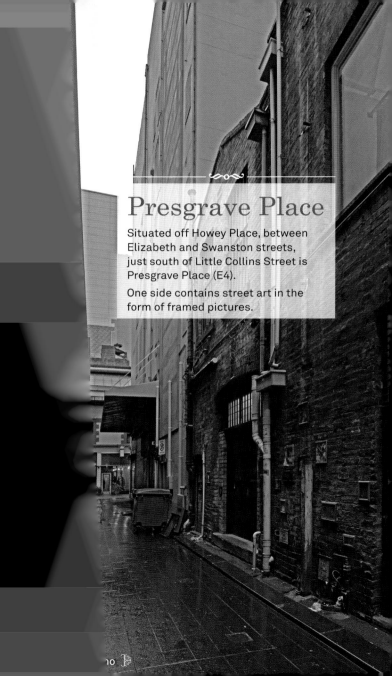

Presgrave Place

Situated off Howey Place, between Elizabeth and Swanston streets, just south of Little Collins Street is Presgrave Place (E4).

One side contains street art in the form of framed pictures.

Princes Walk

Princes Walk is located along the north bank of the Yarra River, east of St Kilda Road, below Federation Square (F6).

The vaults located on the walk were constructed in 1889 and integrate with Princes Bridge. They have been used by businesses since their opening.

Quay Restaurant

Punch Lane

Punch Lane runs north
of Little Bourke Street,
between Exhibition and
Spring streets (H3).

The area was a red-light
district in the late 1800s.

Bluebag Kenny's Bakery Café Longrain Restaurant

Rosa's Kitchen Satchmo's Den Shark Fin Inn

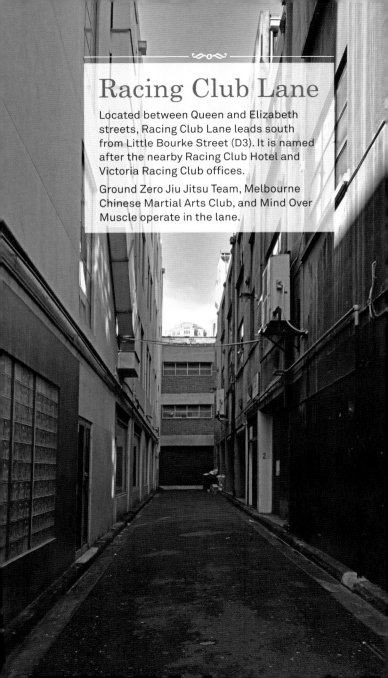

Racing Club Lane

Located between Queen and Elizabeth streets, Racing Club Lane leads south from Little Bourke Street (D3). It is named after the nearby Racing Club Hotel and Victoria Racing Club offices.

Ground Zero Jiu Jitsu Team, Melbourne Chinese Martial Arts Club, and Mind Over Muscle operate in the lane.

Rainbow Alley

Named after the Rainbow Hotel in the mid-1850s, Rainbow Alley is located north of Little Collins Street, to the east of Swanston Street (F4).

The view south shows Council House 2 on the left-hand side. It is the first office building in Australia to achieve a 6 Green Star certified rating.

Also south of the alley is the magnificent Melbourne Town Hall, completed in 1870.

Cabinet Bar & Balcony   Café L'Incontro

Chatter Box   Hairy Little Sista   Sushi Sushi

Rainbow Bridge

This footbridge was completed in 1989 and joins Flinders Walk, near Flinders Street Station, and connects to the Southbank Promenade (D6).

Located under the bridge is Ponyfish Island.

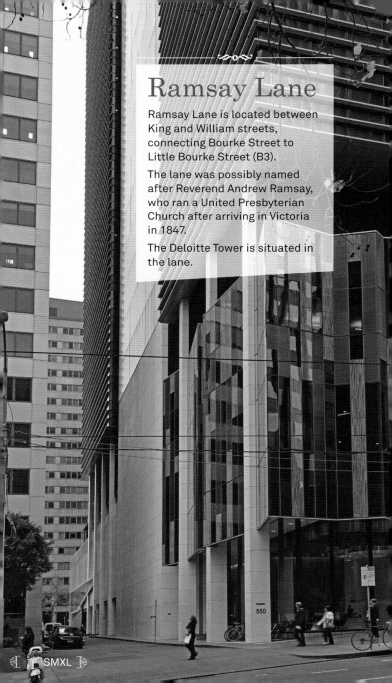

Ramsay Lane

Ramsay Lane is located between King and William streets, connecting Bourke Street to Little Bourke Street (B3).

The lane was possibly named after Reverend Andrew Ramsay, who ran a United Presbyterian Church after arriving in Victoria in 1847.

The Deloitte Tower is situated in the lane.

Ramsden Place

Ramsden Place is located between Swanston and Russell streets, north of Flinders Lane (F5).

It was named in the late 1850s, when wine merchants Dods & Davidson operated from the lane.

The lane leads into the 161 Collins Street arcade in the T&G Building (KPMG House).

Rankins Lane

Rankins Lane is located between Queen and Elizabeth streets, south of Little Bourke Street (D3).

The lane was named after Henry Johnstone Rankine, a cabinet maker.

Factories and warehouses are now residential apartments.

Brother Baba Budan   Gajin Lunch Bar   Manchester Press

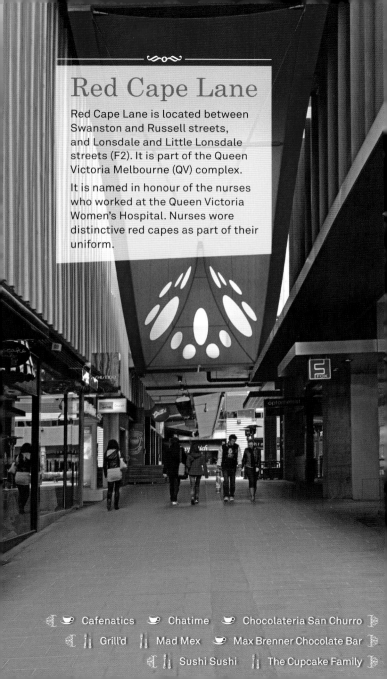

Red Cape Lane

Red Cape Lane is located between Swanston and Russell streets, and Lonsdale and Little Lonsdale streets (F2). It is part of the Queen Victoria Melbourne (QV) complex.

It is named in honour of the nurses who worked at the Queen Victoria Women's Hospital. Nurses wore distinctive red capes as part of their uniform.

Cafenatics   Chatime   Chocolateria San Churro

Grill'd   Mad Mex   Max Brenner Chocolate Bar

Sushi Sushi   The Cupcake Family

Regent Place

Regent Place is located between Swanston and Russell streets, and connects Flinders Lane to Collins Street (F5). It provides access to the Westin Hotel.

It is named after the Regent Theatre at 191 Collins Street, which opened in 1929.

Westin Hotel

Rialto Towers Walkway & Robb's Lane

The pathway between the Rialto Towers and the 'InterContinental Melbourne The Rialto' joins Flinders Lane to Collins Street, located between King and William streets (B5).

The Winfield building is located on the left and the Rialto building is on the right. The Rialto Towers are visible in the background.

Alluvial Bluestone Wine Lounge Cupcake Bakery

Eclipse Café Espressino Hare and Grace Lui Bar

Market Lane Bar Merchant Mr Huang Jin

Nashi Rialto Vue de Monde

Panoramic views can be seen from Vue de Monde, on the Rialto Towers 55th floor.

The luxurious *InterContinental Melbourne The Rialto* incorporates the Winfield and Rialto buildings. The Winfield building was designed by Richard Speight Jr. and Charles D'ebro in 1890. William Pitt designed the Rialto building in 1889. They were warehouses and offices for Melbourne's wool stores in the era of "Marvellous Melbourne". The Rialto Towers were built from 1982-86.

The walkway between the 'InterContinental Melbourne The Rialto' and Rialto Towers displays public art near where Robb's buildings were once located.

Art on display at the InterContinental Melbourne The Rialto', courtesy of James Ridenour.

The 'laneway' located between the Winfield and Rialto buildings is now used by the Alluvial Restaurant and Bluestone Wine Lounge.

Robb's Lane originally
provided access for
wagons delivering wool
to the warehouse, and to
Melbourne's busy docks.
The original winches remain
on the wall.

The lane is located at the
basement level of the
InterContinental Melbourne
The Rialto.

Ridgway Place

Ridgway Place runs from Collins Street to Little Collins Street, between Exhibition and Spring streets (H4).

Senegal date palms and London plane trees peek over the brick wall of the exclusive Melbourne Club, established in 1838.

The Lyceum Club is accessed from the lane.

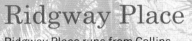

Liaison Café   Lupino   Lyceum Club

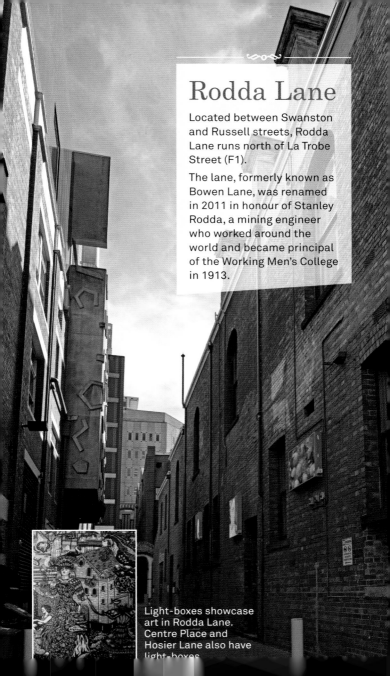

Rodda Lane

Located between Swanston and Russell streets, Rodda Lane runs north of La Trobe Street (F1).

The lane, formerly known as Bowen Lane, was renamed in 2011 in honour of Stanley Rodda, a mining engineer who worked around the world and became principal of the Working Men's College in 1913.

Light-boxes showcase art in Rodda Lane. Centre Place and Hosier Lane also have light-boxes.

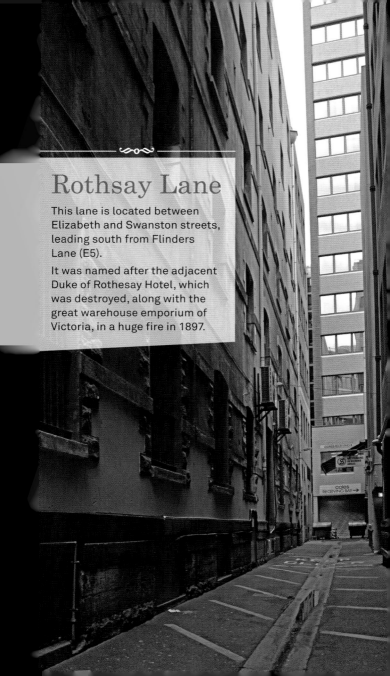

Rothsay Lane

This lane is located between Elizabeth and Swanston streets, leading south from Flinders Lane (E5).

It was named after the adjacent Duke of Rothesay Hotel, which was destroyed, along with the great warehouse emporium of Victoria, in a huge fire in 1897.

Royal Lane

Royal Lane is located between Swanston and Russell streets, north of Little Collins Street (F4).

It was named after the Royal Mail Hotel or the Theatre Royal.

Royal Arcade

Royal Arcade connects to Bourke, Elizabeth and Little Collins streets (E4).

This magnificent arcade was designed by Charles Webb, an architect from England, and construction began in 1869. It was the first arcade in Melbourne.

Caffè e Torta   Kitchen Royale

Koko Black   Suga   The Little Royal

At the northern end of the arcade stands Chronos, a Greek mythological character also known as 'Father Time'.

A feature of the arcade is Gaunt's Clock. Two 2.1-metre-tall statues of Gog and Magog strike the chimes each hour, as they have since 1892.

Gog and Magog are modelled on the figures erected at Guildhall, London, in 1708.

Royal Arcade houses speciality shops among the wonderful architecture.

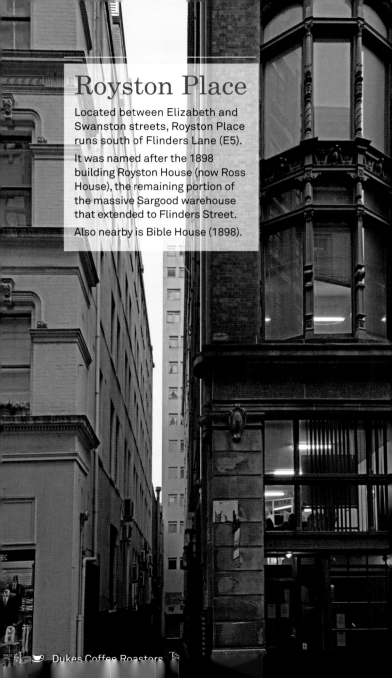

Royston Place

Located between Elizabeth and Swanston streets, Royston Place runs south of Flinders Lane (E5).

It was named after the 1898 building Royston House (now Ross House), the remaining portion of the massive Sargood warehouse that extended to Flinders Street.

Also nearby is Bible House (1898).

Dukes Coffee Roasters

Russell Place

This lane is located between Swanston and Russell streets, from Bourke Street to Little Collins Street (F4).

It is the site of the 1882 Victorian Electricity Company generating station. Melbourne was one of the first places in the world to have a public electric supply.

The Russell Place Substation was rebuilt in 1929, and supplies electricity to the CBD. While it covers half a city block, most people are unaware of its existence underground.

Shown are the Large Mercury Arc Rectifiers that were last in service at the shutdown of the public Direct Current (DC) supply in 2003.

Bar Ampere   Gin Palace   Neapoli   Sarti

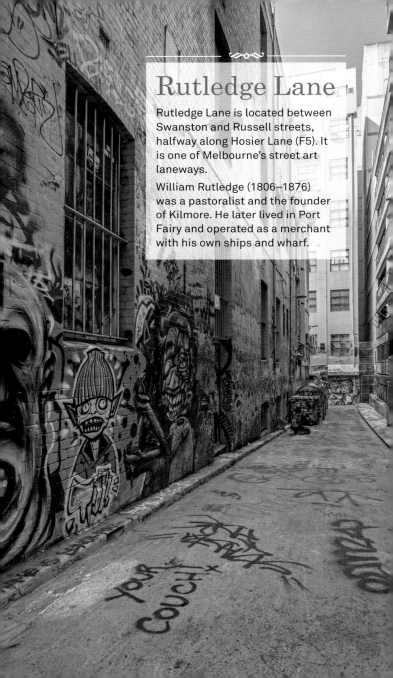

Rutledge Lane

Rutledge Lane is located between Swanston and Russell streets, halfway along Hosier Lane (F5). It is one of Melbourne's street art laneways.

William Rutledge (1806–1876) was a pastoralist and the founder of Kilmore. He later lived in Port Fairy and operated as a merchant with his own ships and wharf.

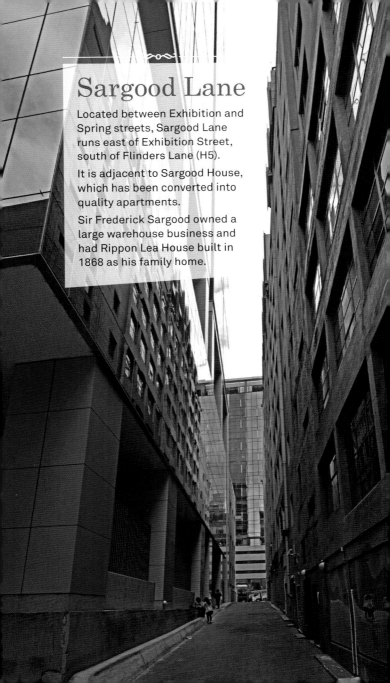

Sargood Lane

Located between Exhibition and Spring streets, Sargood Lane runs east of Exhibition Street, south of Flinders Lane (H5).

It is adjacent to Sargood House, which has been converted into quality apartments.

Sir Frederick Sargood owned a large warehouse business and had Rippon Lea House built in 1868 as his family home.

Scott Alley

This alley is located between Elizabeth and Swanston streets, south of Flinders Lane (E5).

It was previously known as Hotham Place, after Sir Charles Hotham (1806-1855), governor of Victoria from 1854 to 1855.

Singers Lane

The mainly residential Singers Lane is located opposite the Flagstaff Gardens, between William and Queen streets , north of La Trobe Street (C1).

It connects to both La Trobe and Wills streets.

Smythe Lane

Smythe Lane is located between Russell and Exhibition streets, south of Lonsdale Street (G3). It links Lonsdale Street and Cohen Place.

The Aylesbury Restaurant & Rooftop Curry Bowl

Sniders Lane

Sniders Lane is located between Elizabeth and Swanston streets, branching west from Drewery Lane (E2).

It was named after Sniders and Abraham, manufacturing tobacconists.

Street art can be found here.

Sister Bella Bar

Somerset Place

Somerset Place is located between Queen and Elizabeth streets, south of Little Bourke Street (D3).

The lane features creative businesses such as Captains of Industry, Gallery One Three and the House of Jarrari.

During the early 1900s, bicycle businesses and Hatsell King, a cricket bat producer, were located here.

Captains of Industry   The Little Mule

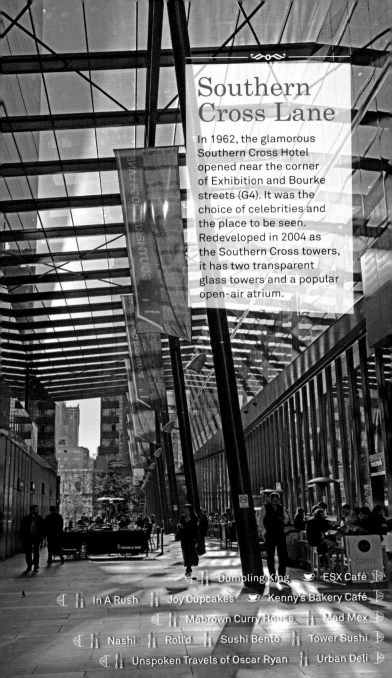

Southern Cross Lane

In 1962, the glamorous Southern Cross Hotel opened near the corner of Exhibition and Bourke streets (G4). It was the choice of celebrities and the place to be seen. Redeveloped in 2004 as the Southern Cross towers, it has two transparent glass towers and a popular open-air atrium.

Dumpling King · ESX Café
In A Rush · Joy Cupcakes · Kenny's Bakery Café
Mabrown Curry House · Mad Mex
Nashi · Roll'd · Sushi Bento · Tower Sushi
Unspoken Travels of Oscar Ryan · Urban Deli

Spark Lane

Spark Lane is located between Exhibition and Spring streets, north of Flinders Street (H5). It is adjacent to the boutique Hotel Lindrum, formerly Lindrum's Billiard Centre.

World professional billiards champion Walter Lindrum held 57 world records, including a break of 4137 in 1932.

In a corner of the lane is a two-storey-high artwork by Mohammed Ali (a.k.a. Aerosol Arabic), who was sponsored by the City of Melbourne and the British Council in 2008 as part of the Melbourne International Arts Festival.

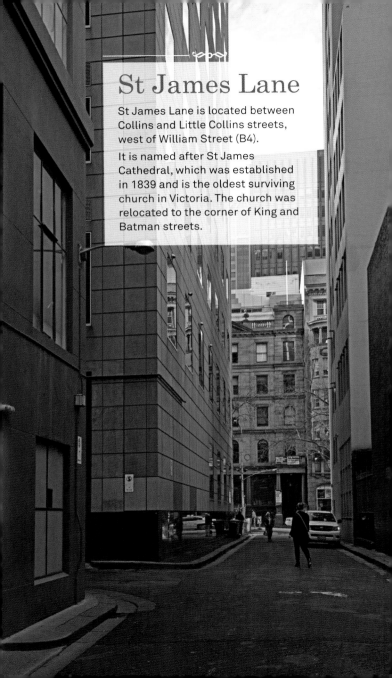

St James Lane

St James Lane is located between Collins and Little Collins streets, west of William Street (B4).

It is named after St James Cathedral, which was established in 1839 and is the oldest surviving church in Victoria. The church was relocated to the corner of King and Batman streets.

St Patricks Alley

St Patricks Alley is located between William and Queen streets, south of Little Bourke Street (C3).

It is named after St Patrick's Hall on Little Bourke Street, which held Victoria's first Legislative Council in 1851 to 1856.

Chi Kitchen

Stall Laneway

Stall Laneway is located between Elizabeth and Swanston streets, north of Little Collins Street (E4).

The laneway is grass covered, with hanging lights and a caravan.

CHUCKLE PARK

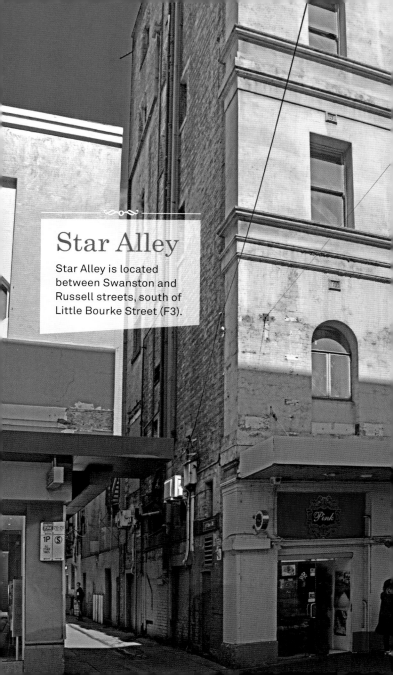

Star Alley

Star Alley is located between Swanston and Russell streets, south of Little Bourke Street (F3).

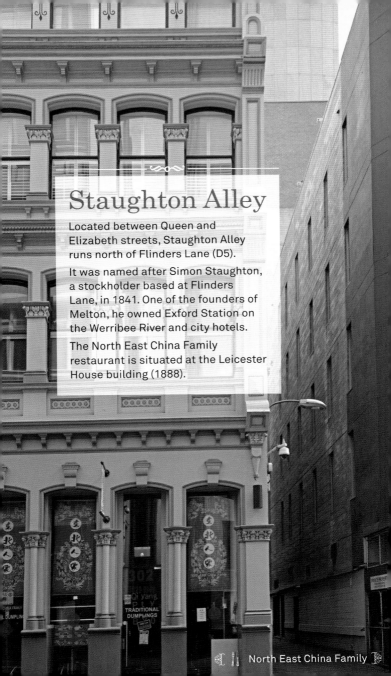

Staughton Alley

Located between Queen and Elizabeth streets, Staughton Alley runs north of Flinders Lane (D5).

It was named after Simon Staughton, a stockholder based at Flinders Lane, in 1841. One of the founders of Melton, he owned Exford Station on the Werribee River and city hotels.

The North East China Family restaurant is situated at the Leicester House building (1888).

North East China Family

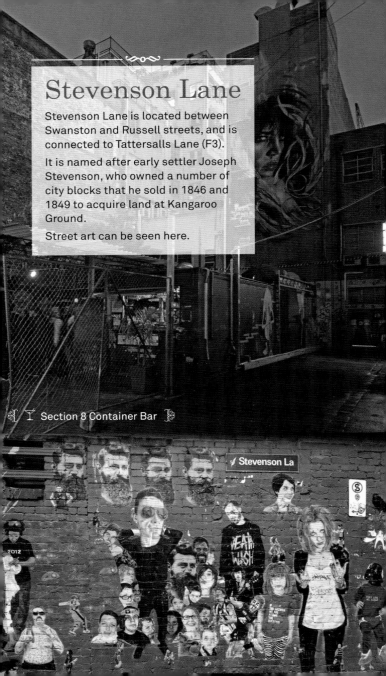

Stevenson Lane

Stevenson Lane is located between Swanston and Russell streets, and is connected to Tattersalls Lane (F3).

It is named after early settler Joseph Stevenson, who owned a number of city blocks that he sold in 1846 and 1849 to acquire land at Kangaroo Ground.

Street art can be seen here.

Section 8 Container Bar

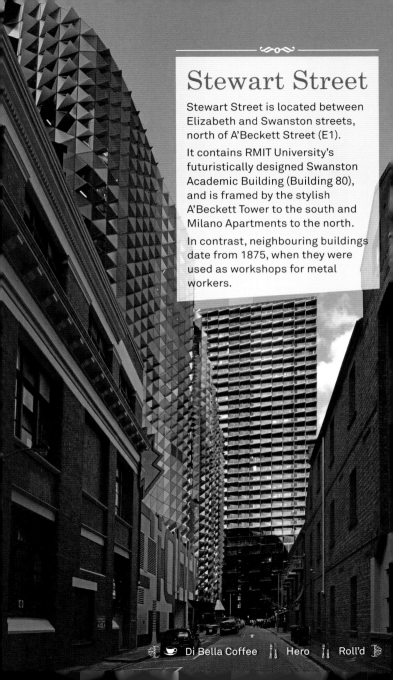

Stewart Street

Stewart Street is located between Elizabeth and Swanston streets, north of A'Beckett Street (E1).

It contains RMIT University's futuristically designed Swanston Academic Building (Building 80), and is framed by the stylish A'Beckett Tower to the south and Milano Apartments to the north.

In contrast, neighbouring buildings date from 1875, when they were used as workshops for metal workers.

Di Bella Coffee   Hero   Roll'd

Strachan Lane

Strachan Lane is located between Flinders Lane and Collins Street, west of Exhibition Street (G5).

James Strachan (1810–1875) came to Melbourne in 1836. His company, Strachan & Co., was a major wool-broker and financial provider that helped the pastoral expansion of Victoria.

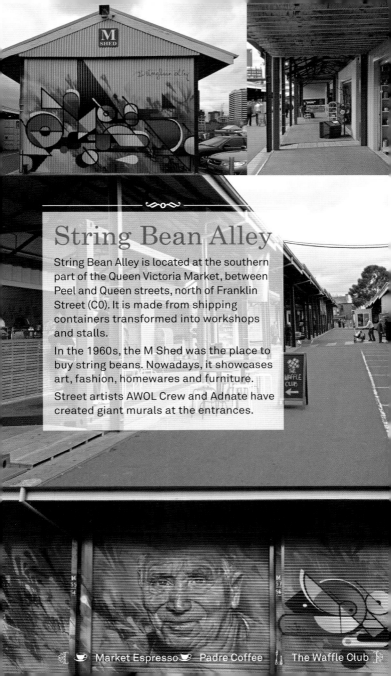

String Bean Alley

String Bean Alley is located at the southern part of the Queen Victoria Market, between Peel and Queen streets, north of Franklin Street (C0). It is made from shipping containers transformed into workshops and stalls.

In the 1960s, the M Shed was the place to buy string beans. Nowadays, it showcases art, fashion, homewares and furniture.

Street artists AWOL Crew and Adnate have created giant murals at the entrances.

Market Espresso ☕ Padre Coffee 🍴 The Waffle Club

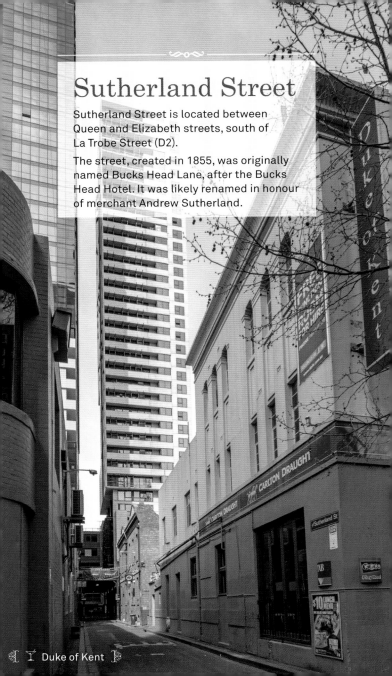

Sutherland Street

Sutherland Street is located between Queen and Elizabeth streets, south of La Trobe Street (D2).

The street, created in 1855, was originally named Bucks Head Lane, after the Bucks Head Hotel. It was likely renamed in honour of merchant Andrew Sutherland.

Duke of Kent

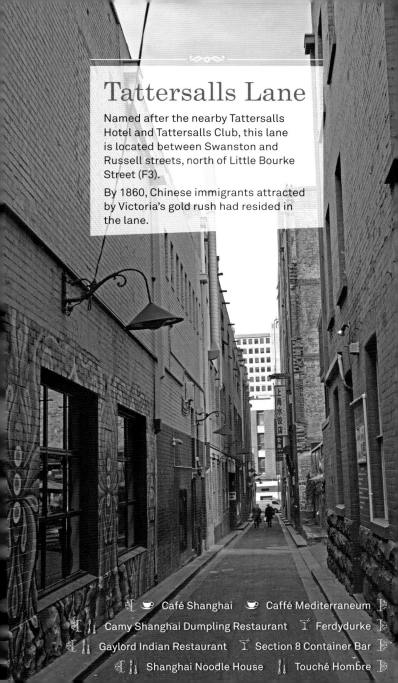

Tattersalls Lane

Named after the nearby Tattersalls Hotel and Tattersalls Club, this lane is located between Swanston and Russell streets, north of Little Bourke Street (F3).

By 1860, Chinese immigrants attracted by Victoria's gold rush had resided in the lane.

☕ Café Shanghai   ☕ Caffé Mediterraneum
🍴 Camy Shanghai Dumpling Restaurant   🍸 Ferdydurke
🍴 Gaylord Indian Restaurant   🍸 Section 8 Container Bar
🍴 Shanghai Noodle House   🍴 Touché Hombre

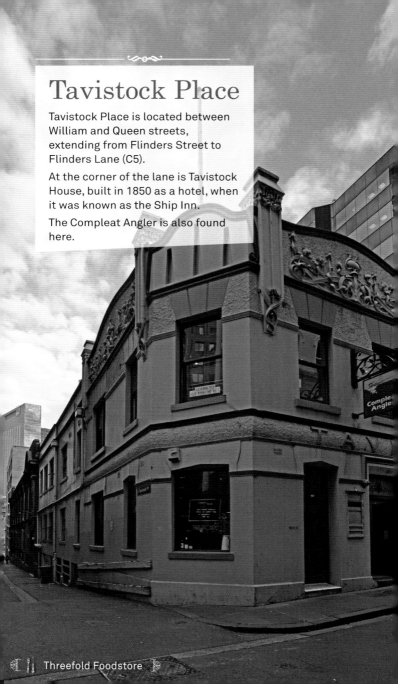

Tavistock Place

Tavistock Place is located between William and Queen streets, extending from Flinders Street to Flinders Lane (C5).

At the corner of the lane is Tavistock House, built in 1850 as a hotel, when it was known as the Ship Inn.

The Compleat Angler is also found here.

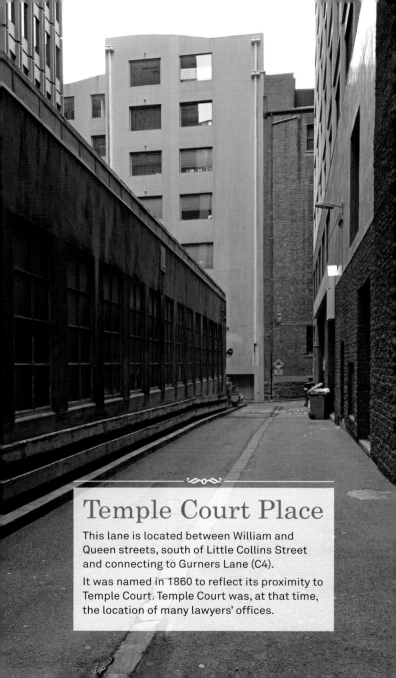

Temple Court Place

This lane is located between William and Queen streets, south of Little Collins Street and connecting to Gurners Lane (C4).

It was named in 1860 to reflect its proximity to Temple Court. Temple Court was, at that time, the location of many lawyers' offices.

The Causeway

The Causeway is located between Elizabeth and Swanston streets, connecting Little Collins Street to Bourke Street Mall (E4).

The lane contains boutique shops and cafés, including the Laurent Boulangerie Patisserie housed in the 1920s palazzo-style Union Bank building.

It was previously known as Craig's Lane, and in 1895 the Mechanics Hotel was located here.

Café Insieme ☕ Gordon's Café 🍴 Grasshopper's Feast 🥢
☕ Kansas 🍴 Laurent Boulangerie Patisserie ☕ Local Birds 🥢
🍴 Malaysian Oriental Wok 🍴 Riva 🍴 Sushi Monger 🍴 Tokio 🥢

Thomson Street

Thomson Street is located between William and Queen streets, south of Little Bourke Street (C3).

It was named after Thomson & Co., brassfounders and coppersmiths, who operated on Little Bourke Street from 1880 to 1950.

Alibi Kitchen & Bar   Ikyu Sushi

Treasury Place

Treasury Place connects Premiers
Lane to Lansdowne Street (I5).
It runs south of the State
Government Offices and connects
to Spring Street, past statues of
former premiers of Victoria.

Turnbull Alley

Turnbull Alley is located between Bourke and Little Bourke streets, west of Spring Street (H3).

It was named in the 1850s and runs along the rear of the Princess Theatre.

Remnants of old housing can still be seen.

Ulster Lane

Located between Collins and Little Collins streets, Ulster Lane leads west from Spring Street (H4).

The lane is near the entrances to the Esanda building and to Parliament Station.

It was named before 1915 after the Ulster Family Hotel on the corner of Little Collins and Spring streets.

Uniacke Court

Uniacke Court is located between Spencer and King streets, north of Little Bourke Street (A3).

The lane contains street art and heritage structures.

A boarding house was situated here during the 1860s.

Street art

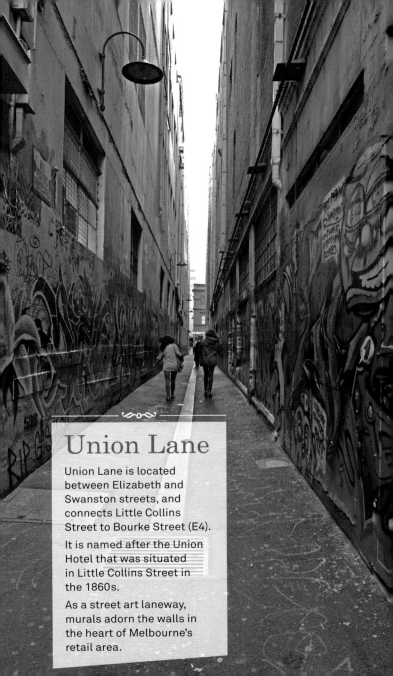

Union Lane

Union Lane is located between Elizabeth and Swanston streets, and connects Little Collins Street to Bourke Street (E4).

It is named after the Union Hotel that was situated in Little Collins Street in the 1860s.

As a street art laneway, murals adorn the walls in the heart of Melbourne's retail area.

Waratah Place

Waratah Place is located between Swanston and Russell streets, north of Little Bourke Street (F3).

It connects Chinatown with the Greek quarter on Lonsdale Street and the Queen Victoria Melbourne (QV) complex.

Blue Sky Café   Exford Hotel   Hot Space Sichuan Bar

International Cakes   Kum Den Chinese Restaurant

Sekai   Stalactites   Yuriya Tepanyaki

Wah Wah Lounge

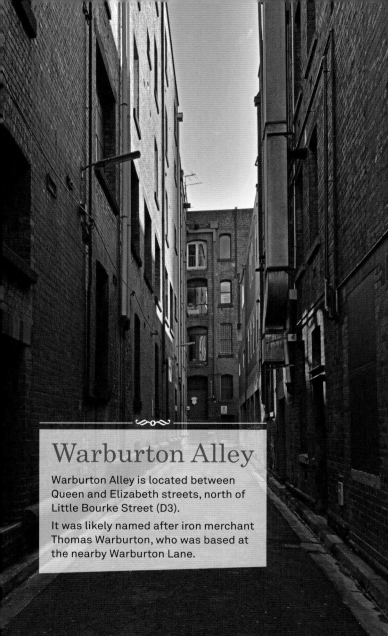

Warburton Alley

Warburton Alley is located between Queen and Elizabeth streets, north of Little Bourke Street (D3).

It was likely named after iron merchant Thomas Warburton, who was based at the nearby Warburton Lane.

+39 Pizzeria & Degustation Bar

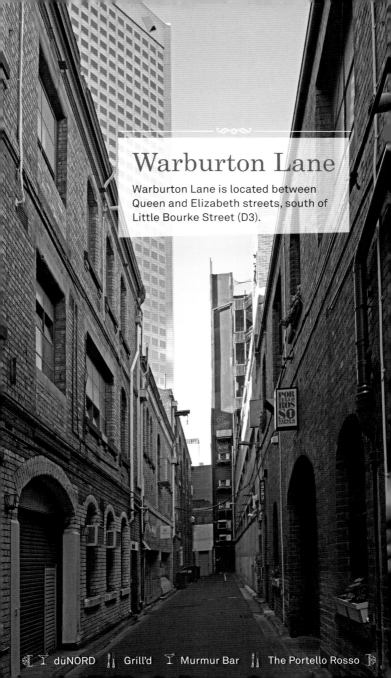

Warburton Lane

Warburton Lane is located between Queen and Elizabeth streets, south of Little Bourke Street (D3).

duNORD   Grill'd   Murmur Bar   The Portello Rosso

Westwood Place

Lying south of Bourke Street, Westwood Place is located between Exhibition and Spring streets (H4).

It was named after James Westwood, who built the Albion Hotel in 1839.

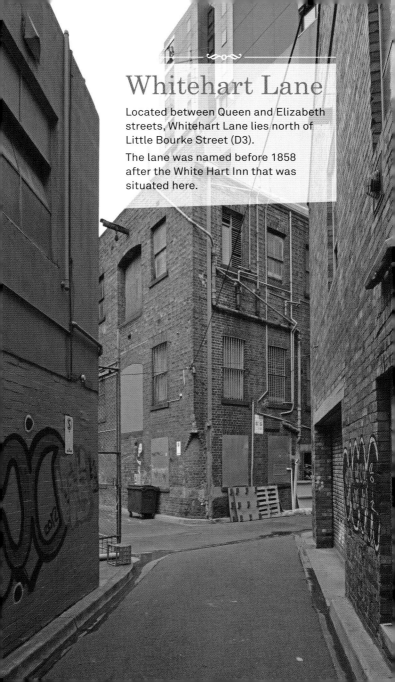

Whitehart Lane

Located between Queen and Elizabeth streets, Whitehart Lane lies north of Little Bourke Street (D3).

The lane was named before 1858 after the White Hart Inn that was situated here.

Wicklow Lane

Wicklow Lane is located between King and William streets, south of Little Lonsdale Street (B2).

The lane's bluestone paving leads past a Federation-era heritage building, along to the bluestone walls of an 1855 building.

History intermingles with the surrounding modern buildings.

Dejavu Bar and Lounge

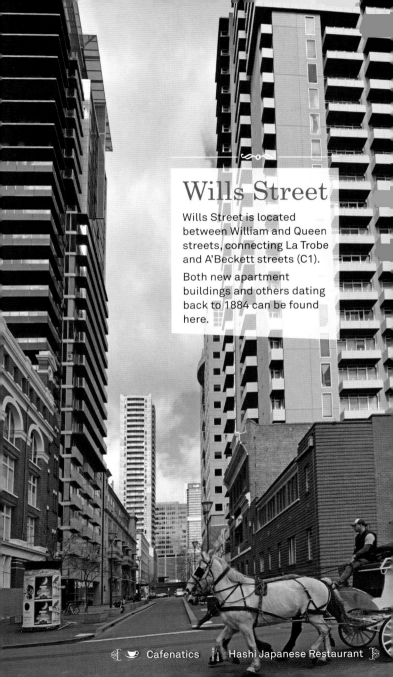

Wills Street

Wills Street is located between William and Queen streets, connecting La Trobe and A'Beckett streets (C1).

Both new apartment buildings and others dating back to 1884 can be found here.

Cafenatics   Hashi Japanese Restaurant

Windsor Place

Previously known as Lang Lane, Windsor Place is located behind the Hotel Windsor (111 Spring Street), between Bourke and Little Collins streets (H4).

The lane was named after the hotel in 1943.

The Hotel Windsor was established in 1883 for George Nipper, a shipping magnate. It was known as 'The Grand', one of the most luxurious hotels in Melbourne, and later as 'The Grand Coffee Palace'.

The hotel was then renamed in honour of the British Royal Family.

Duckboard Club | San Telmo | Wallis & Ed

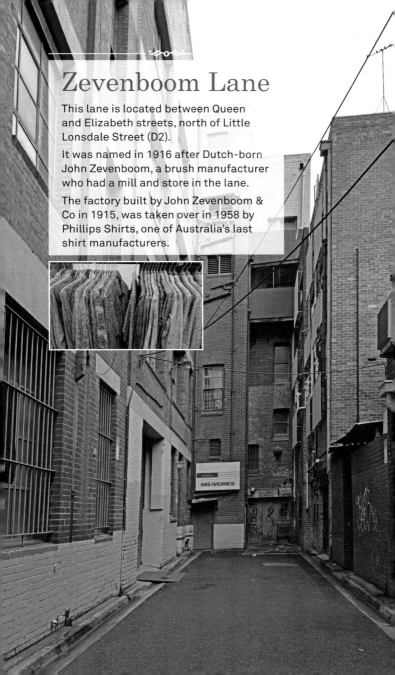

Zevenboom Lane

This lane is located between Queen and Elizabeth streets, north of Little Lonsdale Street (D2).

It was named in 1916 after Dutch-born John Zevenboom, a brush manufacturer who had a mill and store in the lane.

The factory built by John Zevenboom & Co in 1915, was taken over in 1958 by Phillips Shirts, one of Australia's last shirt manufacturers.

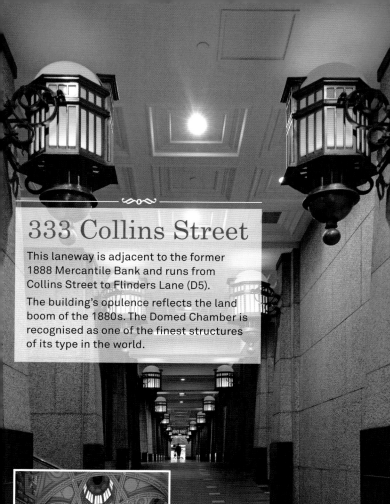

333 Collins Street

This laneway is adjacent to the former 1888 Mercantile Bank and runs from Collins Street to Flinders Lane (D5).

The building's opulence reflects the land boom of the 1880s. The Domed Chamber is recognised as one of the finest structures of its type in the world.

☕ Café Saranti 🍴 Strozzi Caffeteria

Docklands and South Wharf

Webb Bridge

Aurora Lane

Aurora Lane is located in Docklands between Harbour Esplanade and Wurundjeri Way, south of Bourke Street (N5–N7). At the northern end of the lane is Etihad Stadium.

Aurora Lane runs alongside the No. 2 Railway Goods Shed, which was constructed in 1889. At over 385 metres long and 36 metres wide, it was the largest railway goods shed in the state.

Saporo Café

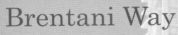

Brentani Way

Brentani Way connects Village Street to McCrae Street, and lies north of the Yarra River (N7).

The façade of the residential tower V1 displays *The Wave* (2006) by Vashti Gonda.

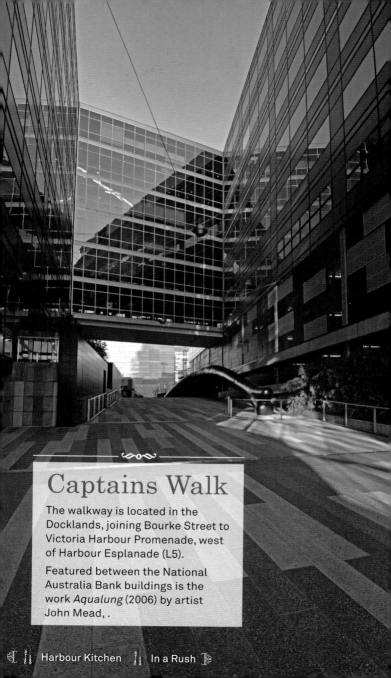

Captains Walk

The walkway is located in the Docklands, joining Bourke Street to Victoria Harbour Promenade, west of Harbour Esplanade (L5).

Featured between the National Australia Bank buildings is the work *Aqualung* (2006) by artist John Mead, .

Central Pier

The historic Central Pier is located between La Trobe and Bourke streets, west of Harbour Esplanade (L4).

The sheds on the pier have been lavishly refurbished.

Victoria Dock was constructed between 1887 and 1892, and is the oldest single large dock still standing in the world. The cargo sheds 9 and 14 were built in 1914. Shed 14 has a 3700-square-metre floor, which is divided into four venues.

Alumbra | MAIÀ | Mill & Bakery | Peninsula

Sketch | Sumac | Va Bene Pizzeria | Woolshed Pub

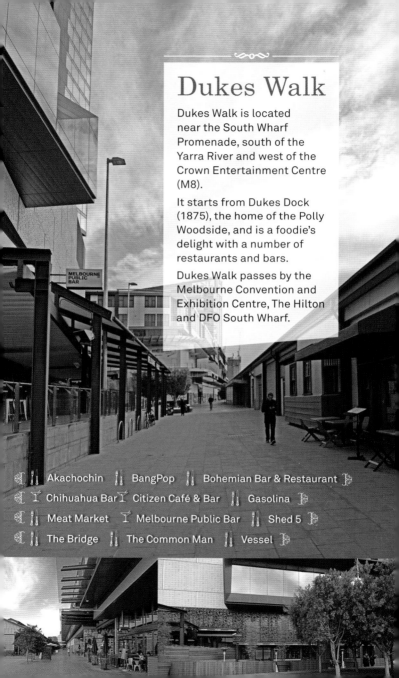

Dukes Walk

Dukes Walk is located near the South Wharf Promenade, south of the Yarra River and west of the Crown Entertainment Centre (M8).

It starts from Dukes Dock (1875), the home of the Polly Woodside, and is a foodie's delight with a number of restaurants and bars.

Dukes Walk passes by the Melbourne Convention and Exhibition Centre, The Hilton and DFO South Wharf.

Akachochin   BangPop   Bohemian Bar & Restaurant

Chihuahua Bar   Citizen Café & Bar   Gasolina

Meat Market   Melbourne Public Bar   Shed 5

The Bridge   The Common Man   Vessel

Fishplate Lane

Located south of Etihad Stadium, Fishplate Lane connects Batmans Hill Drive to Village Street (N6).

A 'fishplate' is a metal bar that is bolted to the ends of two rails, which joins them together.

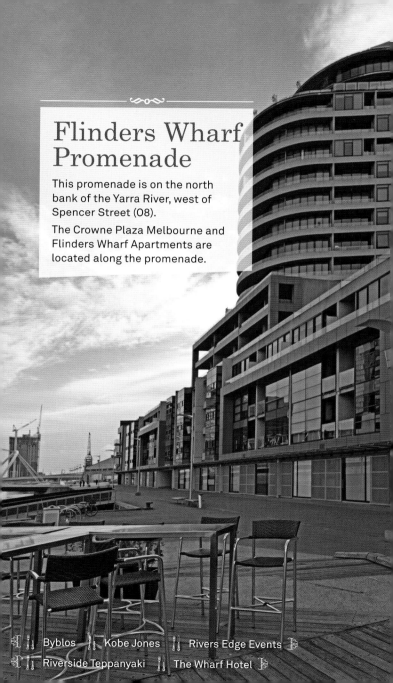

Flinders Wharf Promenade

This promenade is on the north bank of the Yarra River, west of Spencer Street (08).

The Crowne Plaza Melbourne and Flinders Wharf Apartments are located along the promenade.

Byblos | Kobe Jones | Rivers Edge Events

Riverside Teppanyaki | The Wharf Hotel

New Quay Promenade

New Quay Promenade is located at the northern end of Victoria Harbour (J3–L3). A number of lanes run off the promenade, which also leads to a piazza.

All Smiles | Aussie Steak 'N' Burger Bar & Grill | Berth | Bhoj
Dock31 | Fish Bar | Gold Leaf | James Squire
Man Mo | Medici | New Quay International Buffet & Bar
Oscar's Table | Renzo's Bar Café Italiano | Steakhouse 66
The New Quay Hotel | Waterside

Orrs Walk

Orrs Walk is located near the South Wharf Promenade, south of the Yarra River and west of the Crown Entertainment Centre (N8). It divides the DFO South Wharf and The Hilton. Duke's (1875) and Orr's (1878) Dry Docks are nearby.

Charles Orr, Robert Wright and George Duke formed a company that built and operated docks on the Yarra, as well as in Sydney and in Newcastle.

Rakaia Way

Located in the Docklands, Rakaia Way runs south of Docklands Drive, between Doepel Way and Saint Mangos Lane (K2).

Bopha Devi Cambodian Restaurant   Mas Nudle Café   Pho

Rona Walk

Located in the South Wharf Promenade area, Rona Walk connects Dukes Walk to Convention Centre Place (M8). It runs between DFO South Wharf and The Hilton.

The *Polly Woodside* ship at South Wharf had been renamed *Rona* in its early sailing history.

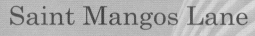

Saint Mangos Lane

Saint Mangos Lane is located between Footscray Road and Waterfront Way in the Docklands (L2).

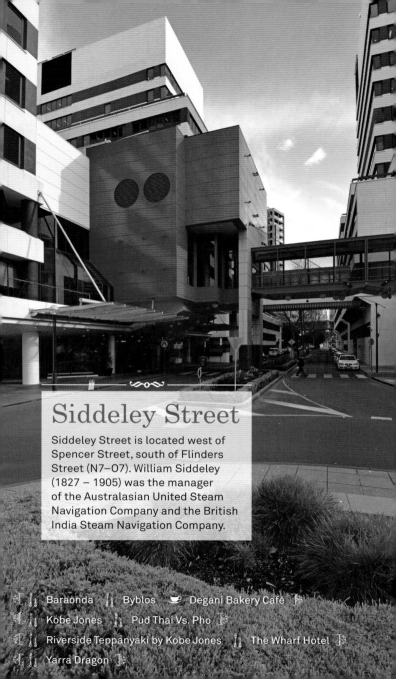

Siddeley Street

Siddeley Street is located west of
Spencer Street, south of Flinders
Street (N7–O7). William Siddeley
(1827 – 1905) was the manager
of the Australasian United Steam
Navigation Company and the British
India Steam Navigation Company.

Baraonda | Byblos | Degani Bakery Café
Kobe Jones | Pud Thai Vs. Pho
Riverside Teppanyaki by Kobe Jones | The Wharf Hotel
Yarra Dragon

South Wharf Promenade

The promenade offers waterside dining along the south bank of the Yarra River in beautifully restored warehouses (M8-N8).

The South Wharf Promenade bypasses the *Polly Woodside*, which is open for inspection.

The *Polly Woodside* is a three-masted iron barque built in Belfast in 1885.

Akachochin | CharlieLovett | Meat Market | Shed 5

Showtime Events | The Boatbuilders Yard | The Bridge

Star Circus

Star Circus connects Pearl
River Road to Waterfront
Way in the Docklands
(J1–K1).

It is located next to the
Southern Star observation
wheel.

Star Circus also contains
Wonderland Park, a fun
park with many attractions
and rides, a Tyrannosaurus
Rex, and the Southern
Star — Australia's only
giant observation wheel.

Burger Monster   Chocolateria San Churro

Chillipadi Mamak Kopitiam   Great Taste

Harbour Town Hotel   Healthy Habits   KFC   Nando's

Subway   Sura Korean Restaurant   The Coffee Club

Star Crescent

Star Crescent connects
Docklands Drive to Star Circus
in the Docklands (J1).

Breadtop | Dlands Café | Groove Train

Le Cirque Fine Foods | Rainbows Icecream Parlour

Sushi Sakura

Studio Lane

Studio Lane is located in Waterfront City, connecting Pearl River Road to Waterfront Way (J1–K1).

The lane is popular with shoppers.

Dlands Café   The Juice Cove

The Arcade

The Arcade connects Waterfront Way to Star Crescent in the Docklands (K1).

VACC Walk

VACC Walk connects Batmans Hill Drive to Harbour Esplanade (M7).

It bypasses the Kangan Institute's Automotive Centre of Excellence.

The artwork featured is *Car Nuggets* (2006) by Patricia Piccinini.

Near VACC Walk is the historic Queens Warehouse (1890), a former customs building, which houses the Fox Classic Car Collection. The collection includes over 50 prestige vehicles donated by trucking businessman Lindsay Fox.

Café La Kiss

Victoria Harbour Promenade

The promenade is located at the southern end of Victoria Harbour (L5). A number of lanes run off the promenade, which has a view of the Bolte Bridge.

Harbour Kitchen   Little Nyonya   Squires Loft

Rise International Buffet & Bar   Tataki   Watermark

Village Street

Village Street is located in the Docklands between Harbour Esplanade and Wurundjeri Way, south of Bourke Street (N5–N7). It runs along the historic No. 2 Railway Goods Shed.

The goods shed was built to float on soaked wooden rafters. The wood slabs stablise the building in the marshy surrounds, and are preserved in water under the building today.

Bob's Steak & Chop House   ☕ Cafenatics   Nine Elephants

Platform 28   Shuji Sushi   11" Pizzeria

Waterview Walk

Waterview Walk connects Bourke Street to Batmans Hill Drive (M5). The tree-lined walkway passes a number of public artworks.

Café de Kikaku   Flavor 7   Gloria Jeans

Meehub Noodle & Sushi Café

Watergate Convenience & Internet Café

Wharf Lane

Wharf Lane connects
Flinders Wharf Promenade
to Siddeley Street (O7).
The lane displays four of
the fish sculptures used
in the Melbourne 2006
Commonwealth Games.

Wharf Street

Wharf Street, located in the Docklands, connects Docklands Drive to Observation Drive (K1).

Chillipadi Mamak Kopitiam   Gloria Jeans

Sandwhich Chefs   The Coffee Club   The Juice Cove

Published by Melbourne Books
Level 9, 100 Collins Street
Melbourne VIC 3000
Australia
www.melbournebooks.com.au
info@melbournebooks.com.au

Disclaimer:
The authors and publisher have used their best efforts to
ensure the information presented is as accurate as possible,
but accept no responsibility with respect to accuracy or
completeness of the contents of this book. They accept
no responsibility for any loss, inconvenience or injury
incurred by any person using this book, or by any business,
individual or organisation featured in this book.

NATIONAL LIBRARY OF AUSTRALIA
CATALOGUING-IN-PUBLICATION ENTRY:
AUTHORS: Freeman, Kornelia. Pukk, Ulo
TITLE: Laneways of Melbourne
ISBN: 9781922129116 (pbk.)
SERIES: Portraits of Victoria.
SUBJECTS: Alleys–Victoria–Melbourne.
Melbourne (Vic.)–Description and travel.
DEWEY NUMBER: 919.451

First Edition: May 2013
Second Edition: December 2013

Portraits of
VICTORIA

I   The Dandenong Ranges
II The Yarra Valley & Surrounds
III Laneways of Melbourne Edition 1 & 2
IV The Mornington Peninsula To Wilsons Promontory

Visit the website: www.portraitsofvictoria.com.au
Laneway tours also available through the above website.